KIDS WE WERE

A Collection of Memories
from
Children of the 20th Century

Written by Bernie Morris Et Al
compiled and edited
by
Bernie Morris

First published in 2007 by Bernie Morris for

Save the Children

2nd edition published 2008
by
Hometime Books

Printed by Lightning Source UK

This edition published 2013
9780957074545
by
Bronwyn Editions
www.bronwyneditions.co.uk

This book is dedicated to the memory of my mother,
Ellen Bennett,
who lived for her children

Acknowledgements

To my family, friends, colleagues and even complete strangers who
have so kindly contributed their time and their stories.

Namely: Ellen Bennett; Tony Bennett; Gary Burne; Gloria Clark; Dave
Clarke; Elizabeth Clarke; Carole Devine; Deborah Ehmann; David
Garrad; Lindsey Golightly; Ami Gray; Graham Hope; Leopold Howe;
Dan Marshall; Peter McKay; Caroline Morgan; Julie Morris; Robert
Morris; Jim Ollerhead; George Palmer; Lawrence Palmer; Elsie Price;
Janie Quittenton; Richard Quittenton; Michael Rowe; Angela Spencer-
Harper; Barbara Tepper; Colleen Thatcher; Tony Tucker; Brian Ward.

Contents

Introduction

This book is simply a collection of childhood memories, all carefully gleaned from family and friends, from all walks of life, and as wide a circle as possible. All stories are true, insofar as memory permits. All contributors are real and were born in the 20th century.

Their ages range from 16 to 87 at the time of telling. Years of birth range from 1906 to 1990. All have been cajoled, prompted, and edited by me.

In some cases, where I received verbal recall, I have edited out most of the strong language. In others, where such expression is relatively mild, I have left it in, so as to keep the natural voice of the storyteller.

This is not a children's book, although older children might find it enlightening to learn about the childhood of their parents and grandparents and even great-grandparents in the ages before mobile phones and computers.

Bernie Morris

An Indian, a Spear and a Blue Car

The day started off like any other day in the school summer holidays – kids naturally finding ways to entertain themselves. We had no computers back then, no videos, nor loads of pocket money, yet we still had fun and adventure which we made for ourselves. I am extremely glad to have been a child of the sixties and not one of today's kids, as I think they are missing out on so much of their imaginative ability.

Okay, I was nine years old and seeking a little excitement, an adventure, or a new discovery.

I walked over to Peter's house after breakfast, as I did most days. Peter was my best friend, three weeks younger than me, and his house was just fifty yards away from mine, which was quite convenient if it happened to be pouring with rain.

'Hi Pete, you coming out?' I enquired as he opened his front door.

'Yeah, sure mate.' He then shouted back into his house, 'I'm going out with Tony!'

His mother responded from the far distant kitchen, like all mothers did way back then, 'OK, behave yourself and don't be late for dinner!'

Well, we all knew what time "dinner" was. Even without watches; it was about the time our bellies started growling – usually about 12.30 to 1.pm. I guess it is called "lunch" these days.

And we were reasonably good and sensible kids, though perhaps not always as careful as our parents would have liked us to be.

Where we going then? Peter asked as we walked away from his house.

'Don't know, what d'you reckon?' I answered, and then began to think of somewhere we hadn't been for a while.

Just then we saw Chris emerging from his front gate across the road.

'All right, Chris?' we said in unison.

'Hi Tone – hi Pete,' he responded.

Chris had three brothers and a sister, I was one of five, and Peter had three older sisters. I guess families were much larger back in the sixties.

'How about going over to the humps and bumps?' I suggested.

'Yeah, that sounds good,' replied Peter. 'Fancy coming, Chris?'

Chris seemed eager to join us, so off we went.

The humps and bumps was a name we gave to a small area of trees and bushes, interspersed with winding footpaths carved out by kids on bikes and those on foot. This land was made up of several mounds and dips, which adults usually avoided. I guess it was just too muddy for them.

After ten minutes at a meandering kids' pace, we arrived and were quite relieved not to hear any other kids' voices, so I guess we had the place to ourselves. Straightaway, we began running up the humps, down the dips, squeezing through bushes and swinging on branches. I chased Peter; Peter chased Chris, and Chris chased me. We were shouting and yelling without a care in the world, but then I burst through a bush, looked up and stopped in my tracks.

There was someone standing on one of the mounds right at the edge of the area, where a wire fence separated it from a school playing field. I could not help staring. This was a beautiful girl of perhaps thirteen or fourteen. She was wearing weird clothes – a sort of brown suede tunic and sandals and her dark hair was tied tightly back. She was staring across the playing field, but slowly she turned to look at me with deep black eyes, her face otherwise expressionless. Now I was quite a confident, happy-go-lucky child, yet there was an air of strangeness about this girl which I found unnerving.

Before I could decide whether to say something or to run away, Peter came bursting through another bush, closely followed by Chris. Both stopped abruptly as they saw me staring open-mouthed at this strange girl and began to remove stray twigs and leaves from their hair. I guess to hide their embarrassment in the presence of a pretty female.

'Who are you?' I then blurted, my confidence suddenly helped by the arrival of friends.

'I am an Indian,' she replied, speaking slowly and calmly.

The three of us looked at each other, then back at the girl. 'What sort of Indian?' Peter bravely asked, though still breathing heavily from his struggles through the bush.

'I am a Sioux,' she replied, still calmly and curtly.

'What are you doing here?' Peter asked again.

'This is my land,' she stated dismissively, then turned those wonderful dark eyes away from us to gaze once more across the school playing field. It was like we weren't there any more.

I looked at Peter and Chris who were both looking nervous and puzzled, which was exactly how I felt. 'Come on!' said Chris, 'let's play!'

So we tried. We continued running up and down the humps and bumps, trying to forget the Sioux Indian who was standing so near. But it didn't work – just didn't feel right. I guess we were all a bit spooked by the presence of the strange Indian girl.

'Let's go somewhere else,' I suggested at last.

Peter and Chris quickly agreed and we ran through the undergrowth back the way we had come in.

'Bye Sioux!' Peter shouted, then we all burst into a sprint, fearing that perhaps the girl could use magic to stop us. We ran for several hundred yards before we finally slowed and caught our breath. Then we couldn't stop talking about the strange girl we had seen.

'There aren't any Red Indians in England,' I logically pointed out.

'Maybe she just meant that her name was Sue,' Chris ventured.

'NO, she definitely said that she was an Indian and that it was *her* land,' Peter added decisively, 'and we were on her land and she didn't want us to be there.'

'Well, I've never seen her before, and I've been over there loads of times,' I said, using my best logic to ease our worries.

'Maybe she was a ghost then,' joked Chris, and we all let out a nervous laugh, then remained silent.

Years later, I saw that beautiful face again on a record label and I sometimes wonder if her greatest hit was not inspired by us: *Running Up That Hill*. Anyway, it doesn't matter now.

'So where are we going?' Chris enquired, after a few minutes of slowing down, catching our breath and feeling somewhat safer.

'I've never been in there,' I said, pointing to a large field on our left.

'That's part of the big house up there, and we ain't supposed to go there,' Chris informed.

There was a large white house, which had been deserted for years, at the top of the field, a good 200 yards from where we stood, and behind the house was what looked like a small wood. None of us had been in the field before, the presence of a small wooden fence being enough of a barrier to deter most children. However, we were all still excited by our recent encounter and were in the mood to explore – also the mysterious quality of the old empty house was intriguing.

'No-one lives here,' confirmed Peter, 'look how long the grass is – and there's no sign of a car!'

That was it. We felt justified in exploring if nobody lived there and we didn't intend any harm anyway – just to have a look.

Chris seemed the most reluctant, but followed me and Peter as we climbed over the bramble-strewn fence and began walking towards the big house.

We weren't really far from civilisation; there was a main road nearby, yet it seemed very quiet in this field – sort of cut off and lonely. A summer breeze wafted the long grass with a soft whisper as we advanced slowly, without speaking. I looked down and saw something black lying in a small furrow. I bent down to get a closer look. It was something made of metal.

'Here, look at this!' I said in a stage whisper.

Peter and Chris came over as I gently pulled away the grass which partly covered the object.

'It's a spear!' shouted Peter; then lowered his voice, guiltily. 'Pull it out, let's have a look.'

I lifted my find out of the grass and stood it upright.

'It IS a spear,' confirmed Chris excitedly. 'We've met an Indian – now we've found a spear!'

In hindsight, I later realised that the object was almost certainly a railing from a large metal gate, the kind that has spikes on top – but to three nine-year-old exploring kids, it was a spear, large as life, no doubt about it.

'It must be six feet long,' said Peter, eyes wide with delight.

'And it's heavy too,' I added, hefting the weight.

'What are we going to do with it?' asked Chris.

We looked at each other uncertainly.

'It's too big to take home,' I confirmed. 'Let's leave it here, then we can tell everyone that we know where there's a spear hidden.'

They liked this idea, so we placed the spear back in its furrow and recovered it with grass.

'There,' I said, satisfied that no-one else would ever find this precious weapon. 'That's our secret.'

We continued walking towards the big white house, feeling even more edgy than before.

'Shall we go back?' Chris voiced the general feeling.

'No, let's go a bit further,' I said, feeling more frightened than I would admit.

'What if there are more Indians around?' whispered Peter.

We stopped and looked around us nervously.

'Don't be silly,' I tried to reassure, 'there're no Indians around here.' But I didn't sound very convincing.

'So where did that spear come from then?' Peter asked with boyish logic.

'Maybe the house is haunted,' Chris suggested.

We really could have done without his last comment. There we were in a lonely place we shouldn't be; we had just met a Red Indian, found a spear, were worried about other Indians hiding, waiting to pounce. And now we had the possibility of ghosts popping out of the walls of an old spooky house.

Peter stepped on a dead branch and it snapped with a crack which echoed like a shot from a rifle. A dog barked, then another joined in. We looked ahead; the barking seemed to be coming from the woods behind the house. We were exposed and clearly visible – didn't dare run towards the house in case the dogs appeared from the woods. There was only one place to go – back across the open field.

'LEG-IT!' shouted Chris, taking control – and Peter let out a terrified whimper. None of us needed further prompting; we turned and ran like we had never run before, praying that savage dogs would not catch us and rip us to pieces.

I irrationally hoped that I had buried the spear well enough not to trip over it in my panic.

It seemed an age before we reached the wooden boundary fence and we were all over it in a second, not caring if we were scratched by brambles. We carried on running, not daring to look back – if the dogs were after us they could scale that fence in one leap. We sprinted across a quiet slip road and onto a grass verge, just a few yards wide, which bordered the main road.

A blue car was coming from the right. I managed to stop my flight a few feet short of the road, and so did Chris, he and I both panting heavily.

But Peter did not stop. He didn't even slow down. His panic carried him straight into the passing car, his head hitting the nearside windscreen pillar with a sickening thud.

Peter never knew what had hit him. He was thrown several yards in the same direction the car had been travelling and landed on the grass verge, where he lay motionless.

Chris and I looked at each other in horrified disbelief, both still panting for breath; then looking at our friend, lying so still on the grass.

'Why didn't he stop?' I demanded, almost crying.

'Don't know,' replied Chris, shaking his head, still staring at Peter's prone form, with his own tears visibly spilling.

I was just a child then, but I knew this was serious indeed. Peter's head had hit the car like a sledgehammer hitting a rock. Was he dead?

The driver emerged from his car and rushed to Peter's body, but didn't dare to touch him. 'I didn't have a chance - he ran straight into me!' he pleaded, looking up at us, eyes filled with fear and remorse.

Other drivers had stopped and approached us, their faces full of concern. A man emerged from one of the houses across the road and said, 'I've phoned for an ambulance.'

How well we suddenly appreciated the presence of grown-ups at that time, whilst we were locked in shock.

One of the drivers asked if we knew where Peter lived.

'Yes, only a few minutes away,' I replied in a shaky voice.

'Do you think you could go and fetch his parents?' he asked.

'Yes, of course,' I answered – and dragging Chris by the arm, who was still staring at Peter in a shocked state, ran off towards Peter's house.

Peter's mother answered the door with a smile, which instantly dropped as she saw me and Chris standing on the doorstep, looking terrified and without Peter.

'Peter's been run over!' I blurted, not knowing how else to convey this devastating message.

'Oh, my God,' she moaned, and began sobbing as she reached for a jacket in the hallway.

'What's the matter, Mum?' It was one of Pete's sisters who appeared in the hallway a second later.

'Peter's been hit by a car,' the mother tried to explain in her haste.

'Is he all right?' the girl enquired of me and Chris.

'Not sure,' I mumbled, as I truly did not know.

The four of us rushed back to the scene of the accident.

Peter was in a coma for a couple of weeks, but amazingly made a full recovery. He and I remained as best friends for several more years, until we went our separate ways. We didn't see too much of Chris after that day. Perhaps he or his parents thought we were dangerous companions – shame really, as we connected so well.

Needless to say, we were all exceedingly careful when it came to crossing roads, especially Peter.

We never did go back to reclaim the spear, though I did try to find it some years later, without success.

As for the Indian girl, none of us ever caught sight of her again – and she remains something of a mystery to this very day.

So, was she really a ghost, or a childish Kate Bush? Or did she just resemble that beautiful recluse? I still don't know, nor will I ever.

But I do know that every time I hear that song, *Running Up That Hill* I think of her.

Tony Bennett (b.1956)

Bloomers

Yes, girls' bloomers

From the age of 15 to 16, black or navy blue bloomers were prominent in my life as I attended Thetford Grammar School with the girls' school right across the road.

It was and is a great school with only 30% of the pupils being townies in the early 1950's – the remainder coming from areas like Wymon, Fordham and Attleborough and from the north east of Watton.

These pupils travelled up to twenty-five miles by train via the very old rolling stock with old fashioned carriages with no corridors and no toilets.

Henry Watson was our Headmaster and morning assembly was quite an occasion. He read a letter from the Divisional Manager of Eastern Counties Railway, based in Norwich, on a very serious matter.

It had been reported to him that girls' bloomers, black, some blue and some white had been collected from the side of the railway lines over a fifty mile stretch thrown out of the window from both sides of the track, this practice had to cease!!!

We knew the Headmistress of the girls' school would be reading out such a letter at the same time. We townies bombarded the boys travelling on the train. What had been going on?

I believe it was a shameful case of "You show me yours and I will show you mine".

My own embarrassment was the build-up to the annual school cross country race. All 220 pupils had to run, but the principal race was senior boys – 15½ to 16½ (with a few aged 17). I played football and cricket for the school and five of us ran in the Norfolk Grammar Schools' annual cross country race. Reg had come 4th, I came 8th and the others were inside the top thirty so we hadn't done badly as a school.

The senior school boys' cross country, there were forty-eight of us; Reg, Terry and I were the favourites. Within the school sporting curriculum this was the big event, and the last of the four races for different age groups of the day.

I packed my shorts and running vest, cleaned my running shoes. At 10.40 am we all went to the gym to change and, to my horror, I realised I hadn't taken my blue shorts from the airing cupboard, but my elder sister's bloomers, used for hockey.

I raced to Bob England, our Sports Master; we all had a look around for any spare pair of shorts with no result, and five minutes to go for the start.

I was left with no option but to run in them, the course being five miles around the Thetford golf course and back.

In the last half mile there were three of us in the lead: Reg, Terry and me. I put a spurt on and drew ahead. To my horror as we came to the back gates of the school, besides boys lined up at the finish there were at least fifty of the girls from the school opposite the road.

I ran even faster and won, highly embarrassed, but Bob England, lent me his track suit top, so when I stood on the podium and took my prize his top came down to my knees.

My sister (Head Girl at Thetford Girls' Grammar) was quite pleased; she didn't want her bloomers back. The rumour got around in both schools, I had done this for a dare. Full of bravado I didn't let on!

Leaving school was quite an occasion and a wrench.

Some boys and girls left at the end of the 5th year, others stayed on for an extra two years to take their A levels and extra exams hoping to go to University.

The schools were 100 yards from the bridge over the river Ouse, whether we were townies or those who came by train, most of us walked over the bridge every day.

It became tradition that the boys would throw their school caps from the bridge into the river on the last day. The Upper Sixth prefects had gold braid over them, but regardless of cost, they went into the river as well.

No one knows how it happened, but over the years the girls' black or navy bloomers were thrown in as well. By the time I left school, to have sixty caps and sixty pairs of bloomers wasn't unusual floating down the river. It appears the modern miss of the mid 50's wasn't prepared to seek her fortune in the wide, wide world wearing bloomers.

Brian Ward (b.1935)

Broken

I was three or four years old and had just been given a new tricycle—probably for my birthday since that is in April and the weather was warm at the time. We lived in a small house on a hill in Charlottesville, VA, and the porch was high above the sloping ground with a sharp drop off the side of it—probably about eight to ten feet high. I was riding my tricycle around in circles on the porch while my mother was at work, and my father was in the living room repairing a clock with all its parts spread out on the coffee table.

Suddenly, the tricycle went off the side of the porch, and I fell to the ground. It was obvious that my arm was broken since you could see the bone about to poke through the skin. My father took me inside and sat me in a chair instructing me to sit quietly until my mother came home from work, which (it seemed to me) was hours later. I must have been in terrible pain, not only from the broken arm but also from my cut chin which required stitches. I wasn't given anything for the pain—just told not to move around. But all I can remember is how *long* it seemed that I sat and watched him repair the clock. (It is entirely possible, though, in retrospect, that it might have been only one or two hours.) I can still see my mother (thankfully!) getting out of a car and coming up the walk. She immediately took me to the doctor in a taxi where I got stitches in my chin, a cast on my arm and admiration for my bravery. I have no idea why my father didn't take me to the doctor (he didn't even come with us), but the lesson I learned that day is that men are not reliable, and it is the woman of the house who gets things done. I know we had no car or phone, and that we were rather poor, but a little child that young doesn't really think of those things when associating behavior. After all, the little one thinks, "If my mother can get a taxi, why couldn't my father do it?" Another association is that the clock was more important than I was.

I have no idea if this event played a part, but my parents were divorced within a couple of years, and my mother, sister and I moved to Washington, DC.

Carole Devine (b.1939)

Champions

My Father was a champion – in the mid 1930's he could speed down Castle Hill in a frying pan in about 70 seconds.

His Grandfather was a tinker who came from Ireland and settled in Norfolk and brought with him a frying pan which would hold enough eggs and bacon for thirty men. This means it was big enough for a grown man to sit in and come down a 100ft hill at furious pace.

I don't know where the other frying pans came from, but six were enough for a race.

Come WW2, my father and most of the other fit men of his age went off to war to serve leaving my mother with two kids in their early teens who were excited as to what was going on.

Thetford, Norfolk was a battle area with fighter and bomber stations around the area.

I don't know whose idea it was but a dozen children, all early teens, hit upon the idea of copying what our fathers did and to race down Castle Hill in a frying pan if we could find the right type.

Joyce Bossy boots, my sister, thought Dad's frying pan might be up the allotment, taken over by an OAP in his absence. We found it propping up a scarecrow, as it had a 3ft handle. Mum cleaned it, greased the bottom and we were ready for action.

Reg and Freddie, other kids, were very good and could race down the hill in about one and a half minutes without any sprains or serious damage. Although we fell out regularly whilst we practised, Joyce and I were determined to do better. We hid our pan near the hill, so didn't have to lug it a mile home and back and we practised every minute we could.

Between us we agreed six boys would race in six frying pans.

Six assistants would help to support their driver, in my case my sister, Joyce.

There were two other girls as well; they were all horrible and bossy but they insisted on being there or they would tell the soldiers camping near the hill what we were up to, and they would probably takeover.

Somehow the Army knew what we were up to and Sergeant. McKay from the Scots Infantry took us under his wing. He sensibly suggested we should have some rules, such as we all had to be between ten and thirteen years old, the two big kids aged about fifteen were ruled out; they had more strength and weight than the rest of us and were coming down the hill eight to ten seconds quicker than us smaller and younger ones.

We were all excited race day was near. Mums greased up our frying pans. They were all in very good condition despite their age; they were made of some sort of iron, the 3ft handles in particular, solid and essential for steering.

My times were good, I was catching up Reg and Freddie fast and fancied my chances.

Come the day and I thought I would have one more practice; I hit a brick halfway down and catapulted out of the frying pan with a damaged shoulder, so I couldn't race.

Up came my sister, Joyce, still a bossy twelve-year-old but very strong.

We had over a hundred people turn up to see the race, a mixture of mums, oldies and army. Off duty was one policeman and one ambulance man.

I was devastated that I couldn't race, but up stepped sister, Joyce, her turn. She was fourth drawn out of six, she was superb and she won.

Everyone clapped; many rushed to her. As the prize was a pheasant, we all enjoyed that at home.

How was I going to live this down losing to my sister!!

How was she so good? She had been practising regularly; that was obviously made easy by the fact the frying pan was located at the bottom of the hill with easy access to her.

For the next five years at school and then family reunions her success was commented at regular intervals. Dad returned from the

24

War in Burma safe and sound, delighted his own reputation as Champion had been furthered by Joyce the Champion!

Brian Ward (b.1935)

Childhood in the 40s

As children, in the wartime years, we often went out all day. All through the school summer holidays we were allowed to roam freely wherever we wanted as long as we did no damage and were 'seen and not heard'. Most adults were kind to us and there wasn't the pollution and traffic to cause the accidents of today's world.

Our mothers would make up our 'dinners' to take with us, rations permitting. We took it in brown paper bags or carrier bags, or if you were lucky you'd be allowed to borrow your mother's shopping bag, leather or raffia-covered, card milk tops bag. The dinner consisted of thick hand cut (before sliced bread had reached Britain) slices of bread spread with either black treacle, syrup, jam, paste, condensed milk, lard with sugar or dripping with salt. A clear glass bottle with a cork or a brown glass beer bottle with a screw top, of cold tea with a small amount of milk, no sugar as rationing wouldn't allow it. It was hot when you started out. You never had butter or marge as you only got 2oz of butter or 3oz margarine per person per week, which was a half pound pack for a family of four. You'd maybe have a piece of fruit if someone's garden or allotment had some at the time. There was only British-grown fruit as the shipping couldn't get through to import anything; oranges, bananas, grapes and such were unheard of. We had no idea what they were like until after 1945 when the war ended.

A favourite haunt was Monkey Island (without monkeys). This was at a very wide part of the Kennet and Avon Canal where it joined the river behind the sluices between Pingewood and Burghfield bridge. We walked from the sandpits in Tilehurst Road, near where we lived, which was approximately three miles. We went through old Southcote along the rough cart track which was Southcote Lane; it was barley, greens or cattle-grazing fields belonging to the Bucknell family. From Bath Road down Circuit Lane, past the old Southcote Manor ruins, under the brick railway bridge at Holy Brook, across the Kennet

Meadows to the rivers and canal. Then across to the Southcote lock, along the canal bank to the sluice gates. The island was in the middle of the widest part of the Kennet river tributary to the south. It was a shrub-covered piece of land with stony slopes; you were able to swim around it and across to it but you had to keep your 'daps' on (plimsoles, pumps or gym shoes) or you'd cut your feet on sharp stones or broken glass. I did once.

It's much more dangerous now as it's deeper with more weeds as it doesn't get dredged for the barge traffic that used it regularly for carrying freight. Even so a few children were drowned there by not taking care.

Along the Burghfield Road towards Reading, over two bridges built together, one over the railway line, one over the Holy Brook. The latter is an arched, brick-built one with a shelf across about halfway up, above the water. We used to swim and picnic here. The water was so clear and sparkling, you could see the stones and weeds and count the fish. I used to think this was why it was called the Holy Brook until I learned about the Reading Abbey and how the monks used it for water before and after they built the abbey. This was where they originally settled, where the brook ran into the river Kennet at Chestnut wharf in town, near the ruins.

The Cunning Man public house, now a café, was at the Pingewood Road crossroads. Opposite was The Swan (now taken the name *The Cunning Man)*, a pub that had a long veranda at the front with wooden steps up to the doors.

It was set in lovely cottage gardens. Between 2pm and 7pm when it was closed to the public, the landlord would fill your empty cold tea bottle with water and let you sit on the veranda steps to drink it.

The same went for the railway signal men at Southcote signal box, as they had an outside tap at the bottom of the wooden steps. We would try to be there when my father (he was a steam engine driver) was on that Basingstoke line. We would stand with our feet through the iron railings and wave and cheer as he sped past, he would see us and when we were all home used to tell us never to go on the line itself or we'd be killed.

We collected wild flowers as there were so many then, you were allowed to. We took bunches home to our mothers and neighbours. There were loads of them, cowslips, anemone, primroses, bluebells, harebells, campion, cuckoo flowers, meadowsweet, bulrushes, irises, too many to name, but my favourite were the turkey caps. There were masses all over the Kennet water meadows where the Kingfishers darted by the Milkmaid Bridge, a white-painted wooden, arched bridge over the Kennet where it ran into the Kennet and Avon Canal, just down from the Southcote Lock.

We picked vegetables for Farmer Bucknell. He would weigh them and give us so much a bushel. He would let us take a small amount home in our saddle bags and pay us for what we had picked; I don't remember how much but it wasn't a lot. There were broad and runner beans, marrows, cabbages, brussels, cauliflower, salad stuff, anything that grew above ground. Mostly they were grown in the walled kitchen gardens that belonged to the old Coley Park Mansion that had been destroyed in the civil war. The Royalists and the Roundheads had fought all over the area and it had changed from one to the other so often I don't think they could have recorded it all. There were only the barns and a big round dovecote left; they still exist near the old farmhouse but they've been turned into new housing. The present Coley Park House was built some considerable time afterwards and is now used by a private hospital for outpatients. So much has changed or just simply gone forever, a lot not for the better.

Reading was a small town then, surrounded by fields, farm and woodland. There are still a few unspoilt places where you can take a pleasant rural walk, but these are rapidly diminishing to make way for industry and housing. Whenever I chance upon one of these oases on a sunny day, I can still feel with nostalgia, the heat of the sun on the dusty dried ground, the scent of vegetables, flowers and fruit. The droning of the bees and insects, from a lifetime away...

Colleen Thatcher (b.1937)

The Love of Cricket

Norfolk is not an area associated with County and International Cricketers and yet always having a good minor County team traditionally playing at Lakenham, Norwich — some schoolboys have progressed to become well known Internationals.

In the late 50's and 60's I played Grammar School cricket and then for the County with Peter Parfitt, our Captain, John Edrich, both of Middlesex and both went onto play for England for many years. Another name in that era was David Later, a fast bowler who went to play on for Northampton.

Thetford Grammar School had a benefactor who paid for some of us to watch Cambridge University at Fenners and then a Lords Test Match against Australia.

To go to Fenners (Cambridge University Ground) in the 50's and 60's was an honour.

The team the University had in those days was equal to a full blown County side as many players went onto play for their Country.

In the 50's the Team included:-

  , Sheppard
  , Dewes
  , Doggatt
  , PBH May (later an England Captain)
  , Ramon Subba Row
  , Robin Marlor
  , Kuan McCarthy (South African Fast Bowler)

Remiss of me I can't recall the remainder of the Team at that time – they could certainly give any County side a run for their money.

One other distinctive player years later was JJ Warr who went on to play for Middlesex and England and, of course, Ted Dexter, Sussex and

England Captain followed him.

Our trip to Lords on a Friday, the second day of the Test against Australia was incredible, Len Hutton was 101 not out and Tom Graveney ninety-seven overnight. What better could you possibly have as a base for a marvellous day's cricket?

These memories of a schoolboy was a base for a love of cricket that has never waned. My own achievements were modest compared to those mentioned above playing in the London circuit. I was a modest achiever, but do remember one game against the BBC at Motspur Park, Brian Johnson the famous BBC Presenter and Cricket Commentator was their Captain: a legend in his own right. He kept wicket, he kept a running commentary of jokes and stories which as a Batsman you couldn't resist listening to. He must have got dozens out over many years – more than the Bowlers.

Modern Cricketers would never have heard of Gentleman and Players. The era was 50's and 60's where the difference between the workers and the toffs was distinctive in the team and on the playing field. Think of Fred Trueman, (Yorkshire) and Brian Statham (Lancashire) – one of the best opening Bowler partnerships ever seen as the men from the Pits and Peter May and Colin Cowdray (Oxford University, Kent and England Captain) as the aristocrat captains. I gather off the pitch the segregation continued in the hotel, staying overnight, even with the transport to the ground.

Gradually this ridiculous situation lapsed and teams became teams in every sense of the word.

How do we compare the present era with that of the past? England's success over Australia, partially Sri Lanka and the last Test against India is because they are a team They hunt as a pack: a newspaper expression but true. Twelve or thirteen men trust each other and play off each other. Success breeds success: a good old fashioned expression which is still true today.

Then look back to the 60's when Harold Larwood bowled bodyline in

Australia. Years later, John Snow bowled with equal venom, so Ray Illingworth and his team won a test series in Australia.

A cricket historian will think of Lillee and Thompson for Australia and the West Indian period of dominance with four of the fastest bowlers hunting together.

What is so special about Test cricket? It lasts for five days. How do you explain to an American guest who came to a Lords Test with me? You can play a game for five days and still have a draw?

Brian Ward (b.1935)

Cross Purpose

Hi, I'm Deborah from the good old U.S of A.

As a child, I went to Sunday School at Alpha Baptist Church. The entire class, many groups of different aged kids, were offered a prize: a cross pendant on a chain for the girls, and something else for the boys that I had no interest in. I wanted that cross pendant real bad! I was the shy one in my group, so had to confide to the teacher. I said, 'I want that cross.'

The cross was so different and unusual. If you looked into the middle of the two cross beams, you could see the 23rd Psalm. I couldn't even read much yet, but I wanted that cross with all my heart.

The teacher must have been in shock and said she hoped I'd get it, but I would have to work very hard. She said there were a lot of other girls who wanted it too. She wrote a note for each of the kids in my group to give to their mothers. I didn't need a note; I could remember to tell my mom I had to memorize the 100th Psalm, and had two weeks to do it. My mother was quite annoyed because I asked her to read me the 100th Psalm repeatedly.

The next Sunday, a week before the time limit for the contest was up, I went to my group in Sunday School. The lady who always spoke began to speak again, and everyone had to sit and listen.

I listened and then she mentioned the cross pendant and the contest. I stood up, went to my teacher and told her I already knew the 100th Psalm.

She said, 'Sit down Debbie, we will talk later.'

I said, 'No, I know the 100th Psalm.' I was afraid another kid would get that cross ahead of me.

She smiled then and said, 'Whisper it in my ear,' and I did.

Teacher raised her hand and said, 'Our group has someone who already knows the 100th Psalm.'

Then the worst thing of all happened. I had to go to the front of the room and stand on a table so everyone could see me.

I couldn't speak. Everyone was looking at me, and I was shaking with fright. I think my teacher must have done this to teach me a lesson, and it certainly did.

Then she asked me, as she came closer, 'Debbie, do you want this cross?' She showed it to me, glinting in her hand and suddenly I closed my eyes. There, in my head, I saw the 100th Psalm just as if it were written on a scroll all in shining gold letters. I didn't need to look at the class as I said the 100th Psalm.

All people that on earth do dwell
Sing to the Lord with cheerful voice
Him serve with mirth, his praise forth tell
Come we before him, and rejoice.
Know that the Lord is God indeed
Without our aid he did us make
We are his folk, he does us feed
And for his sheep he does us take.

O enter then his gates with praise
Approach with joy his courts unto
Praise, laude, and bless his name always
As it is right, for us to do.
For why? The Lord our God is good
His mercy is for ever sure
His truth at all times firmly stood
And shall from age to age endure.
To Father, Son, and Holy Ghost,
The God whom heav'n and earth adore,
From us and from the angel host
Glory and praise forever more!

Everyone clapped. I had won the cross, and was the happiest kid in the world. I learned right then that you can trust your mind rather than your nerves – or maybe God?

Deborah Ehmann (b.1954)

Egg on Toast

I attended St Michael's RC junior school situated at George Leigh street situated in Ancoats central Manchester, just off the Oldham Road and Ancoats Street. Those were austere years indeed just after World War 1.

At a young age I contracted scarlet fever. No antibiotics were available back then and the disease had progressed enough for me to need an operation to remove half of one of my lungs. My parents were relatively well off and could afford a good surgeon, a luxury most kids were not privy too.

I have to smile now when I look back on that episode as after the operation my parents were given strict instructions to feed me up. Only the best cuts of meat with huge chunks of fat still attached were to be eaten for my speedy recovery!

Fatty meat or not I have been ever grateful to that surgeon and the fact that my parents could afford to pay for my life saving operation.

In 1926 (the year of the general strike) another occasion in particular that reflected those bleak years comes back to my mind.

The school was divided into three distinct levels or *standards* (1 to 6) for ease of access and also for the segregation of the three age groups that attended.

On this occasion I attended standard four. The first floor was for the infants, the second floor was for the girls only and my classroom was located on the third floor.

Playtimes were taken outside in the street as the school didn't possess a playground. Most traffic consisted of the horse and cart with little motorised vehicles being present. The huge shire horses were gentle giants indeed and pulled huge loads with little complaint. A system of two giant beasts (called chain horses, due to the heavy tethering chains) dragged monstrous loads past our school and we would sometimes dart across the street in front of the huge legs of the proud animals purely for *devilment.*

During the winter at lunchtimes, me and a gaggle of hungry children descended a wide stone and iron supported spiral staircase past the second and first floor levels to the warm and welcoming six inch in diameter feeder pipes that led from the boiler house to the giant cast iron radiators for the entire school.

I was fortunate enough to live with my four elder brothers in a public house, my father (Sam Marshall) being the landlord of the Crown and Anchor in Hilton street Manchester, one of the oldest pubs in central Manchester. Originally built in 1793, the building still stands and is used as a pub today.

I found a cosy seat on the heating pipes and carefully unwrapped my lunch to find two thick slices of toast with a delicious centre of a poached egg. I raised the tempting wedge of thick sandwich to my mouth to take a huge bite when out of the corner of my eye I spotted a very dishevelled looking waif, bare footed (which was normal for the time, with many children not having the luxury of a breakfast before leaving for school) and dressed in a sorry state indeed, with a raggedy shirt and torn short trousers exhibiting the tell tale signs of many years of hand me down use from older brothers being at least two sizes bigger than the poor lad needed to cover his painfully thin body.

He stood there looking enviously at my sandwich lunch with a look of mournful hunger on his face. I instantly took pity on this lad and offered him half my sandwich which he gratefully accepted, lunging for the egg and bread and stuffing the whole lot in his mouth at one go!

The next and following days he was there again!

Some days when I opened my lunch the egg had been replaced by bacon or succulent sausage. I sometimes managed to bring extra to share with him until the day came when the young lad didn't come to school any more. I never knew what had happened to him but left St Michaels shortly afterwards myself to go to secondary school.

Most nights after school and weekends I worked in the pub bar with my father pulling pints and, bottling draught Guinness in the cellar with my four older brothers.

Dan Marshall. b.1917

Elizabeth

She wasn't a bully as such, because she really meant no harm to anyone, but Elizabeth was the most irritating twelve-year-old classmate you could imagine. Her forté was practical jokes or just general teasing and she excelled at both, much to everyone's annoyance. That's not to say the rest of us were a miserable bunch without any sense of humour – far from it. But you can have too much of a good thing and Elizabeth just didn't know when to stop.

In class, she would ping elastic bands at all and sundry – sometimes even at the tutor when her back was turned, and when the irate teacher demanded to know who had done it, she never owned up, and it was a kind of unwritten rule in those days that you never grassed on a schoolmate. She often earned detention for the whole class.

If she were standing behind you in assembly when we were required to attend in straight lines and keep absolutely quiet, she would plait your hair and arrange it into all kinds of weird and wonderful styles, while you didn't dare protest for fear of attracting attention of the headmistress who was speaking from the stage. So you had to put up with looking like Medusa until you were safely out of the hall.

She used to ask the teachers loaded questions, like when we were studying Homer's *Odyssey*, she might say, 'What does "lay with" mean?' Of course we all knew very well what it meant and that she was just trying to embarrass the tutor. Nevertheless, some of the teachers' red faces and stilted explanations provided a few giggles.

But one time, she played a nasty trick on a teacher which left us all cold.

Miss Tobin took us for English and it was known that she suffered from stress and was a nervous type although she was a very kind lady. She had often been seen rummaging in her handbag for a pack of cigarettes, then remembering where she was and hastily putting them back.

On this particular day, Elizabeth set up the teacher's desk, which was raised on a dais, so that the two front legs of the table were barely perched on the edge of the platform and with the slightest pressure, they would fall. No-one tried to stop her at the time, although some of us were unsure if this would be wise.

Miss Tobin entered the room and greeted the class. We greeted her back, 'Good morning Miss Tobin.'

She sat down at the desk and said, 'Take out your English books,' in the usual fashion. Then she placed her elbows on the table. As expected, the two front legs of the table immediately crashed from the platform onto the floor. Then the desk toppled over entirely, splashing ink, papers and pens all over the pupils in the front row.

Miss Tobin remained on her chair for a moment or two, white-faced, aghast, and stunned with shock. Then she just keeled over and fell off her chair. She had fainted.

As you can imagine, none of us felt particularly heroic at that moment, although one or two of us ran to fetch help, as the initial spurt of laughter quickly died. I believe Miss Tobin survived this incident, though I am not sure if she ever taught again.

So, Elizabeth had a lot to answer for, even though she was not always alone in her efforts. She also learned to pick on more resilient victims – those who could take it without making a song and dance (as she called it); those like me, the original muggins.

Thereafter, once she had decided that she "liked" me, I was her chosen target, though definitely not the only one. I tolerated her pranks with as much humour and forbearance as I could muster. On the hockey pitch, she would skilfully trip me over with the stick – that was her idea of a tackle. She knew how to save this tactic until the very last moment and make it look like she had missed her shot and that it was in no way a "foul". When our trainer, Miss Plummer blew the whistle of disapproval, it was usually to berate ME for being such a clumsy idiot and ending up with my face in the mud.

Ours was a Catholic grammar school entirely run by an order of nuns and specially selected teachers. Once a year, we had to undergo a "retreat of silence" for one day – a day for each grade year of the school. When it came to the turn of the 3rd year pupils, it happened to be a lovely sunny day, so we were allowed to take our retreat in the school garden. We weren't permitted to speak, not even whisper. We were supposed to read holy books and communicate only via these, or else with looks or hand signals.

As you can imagine, I felt a bit uneasy when Elizabeth came over to sit beside me on a bench beside a rose bush. Call me a guilt-ridden sceptic, but I couldn't help wondering what she was up to now. Her eyes indicated the book she was holding, in a plain brown paper cover, with a gold cross on the front. She opened a certain page and handed it to me. Then she suddenly moved away, leaving me with the book. I read a few lines out of sheer curiosity; then gasped with amazement at what I was reading.

This instinctive reaction of mine attracted the attention of Sister Monica, who was supervising us. She came bustling over and grabbed the book out of my hand. I felt my doom was sealed right then. It was *Lady Chatterley's Lover...*

But the last straw came one day when we were marching down three flights of stairs to the next class, and Elizabeth was behind me as usual. After pinging my bra strap several times with no noticeable reaction, she actually stuck a pen-nib, or something sharp into my bottom. This was just about the end of the tether for me. I just turned around and clocked her one. I didn't really mean to hurt her, but I kind-of instinctively delivered a karate chop to her collar bone. Just before she collapsed, she said, 'Oh Bern, I never thought–'

That's the trouble, I thought – you never, ever thought.

Two prefects immediately grabbed and arrested me. 'Don't you know how dangerous that is?' one asked me. I didn't know, nor did I care at that moment. I only knew that I was fed-up with Elizabeth's tormenting. I guess I got away with it because she didn't have the nerve to complain unduly. She almost got me expelled; she ruined my reputation at school. Yet all along I knew she didn't mean any harm. My conscience still haunts me sometimes...

Bernie Morris b.1946

Elsie's Exciting Day Out

My mother, Elsie, was born in 1906. She had an exciting day out when she was about five years old that she always remembered.

She lived in the children's section of the local workhouse. Once a year, a charity gave the children a summer treat. This was usually a trip on one of the farmer's horse-drawn Wincanton Haywains. It was normally a picnic at a countryside picnic ground. This particular year they were to be taken to Stourhead Gardens and Tower. It was the talk of the orphanage for weeks before the time of the trip. All were excited about what they imagined it would be like going up the tower and the picnic they would have.

The day dawned a bright summer's day. Everyone had a really hurried 'good wash' with the *Lifebuoy* soap and dressed quicker than usual. The Haywain trundled up the stony driveway, right up to the big front door on time.

They seemed a long while getting the picnic things into the centre of the cart. All the children sat around the edges, with the boxes and baskets at their feet, in their black laced shoes with freshly ironed laces. The boys were in knee-length grey surge trousers held up with braces. The girls had calf-length grey dresses with white pinafores.

The glossy chestnut coat of the carthorse, with his shiny brasses, was a lovely sight. He stopped pawing at the ground as his driver urged him forward, with his excited passengers aboard, out onto the road and on their journey.

They travelled the roads and lanes of Somerset with high hedgerows, going through the middle of two or three villages, waving at people who were going about their business. They came at last to a pair of large iron gates standing open, as if waiting for them. The drive was very long with a large house in the distance. Away up on the right-hand side they turned and there, standing tall and magnificent, stood a large stone tower.

The driver placed chain-held chocks under the iron-rimmed wooden wheels of the cart and gave the horse his bag of hay and a bucket of water.

Meanwhile the children were running and playing games with balls, hoops and ropes, enjoying the sunshine and freedom.

After sometime they were all lined up in twos in a 'crocodile', ready to go up inside the tower. Elsie had thick black hair and large blue eyes in complete contrast with her best friend. Gladys was a lot taller and fair. All the boys and girls had their hair cropped short as possible to keep them clean. It also distinguished them in school from the other town children with whom they were not allowed to associate. There they all stood, hand in hand, waiting to go. This day was for fun.

They moved slowly forward with the helpers and made their way up the stone staircase. A little way up, they could see the glow of the sun streaming through the pink glass at the top of the tower. At this moment, Elsie's knees buckled and her head seemed to whiz around; she couldn't get her breath. She felt as if she were falling. She didn't know what vertigo was. Luckily, one of the helpers, Miss Green, caught her as she was falling and got her back down to sit on the bottom of the steps, as she went back to deal with the others. Elsie sat rooted to the spot till they all returned and she never did see the tower and the view. The others were talking about it for a long time after; even years later, when she met Gladys again, they talked about it.

They spread all the rugs under the trees. The helpers gave out bottles of home-made lemonade and ginger beer that they drank with sandwiches, rock cakes and sugary bath buns. It was all soon gone; they then played organised games like, *Sheep, Sheep come home*, *Statues* and *Hide go Seek*.

Time to leave soon came round. Everything was piled again into the centre of the Haywain, and they all took their seats. By now they were quite tired. They sang folk songs as they rode, but then fell asleep leaning on one another. With the setting sun shining through the trees, they clip-clopped homeward to the big old house built of Willet Stone.

Elsie Price (b.1906)

First Life of Lun

I don't remember much of this except for the scary bit; I had to glean information from my older brothers and my mum, so please bear with me.

I was born in 1975, the Chinese year of the Cat, so my mum always reckoned that I should have nine lives. Well then, I guess this was my first narrow brush with death:

I was two years old and had been put to bed with my bottle and teddy about an hour before my brothers came up. Mum always sang me a song or told a story, so I guess I was lucky like that. After she kissed me goodnight, I dozed for a bit.

But then an hour later, my boisterous brothers were also sent to bed, so came upstairs to our shared bedroom. I woke up, as I greatly enjoyed listening to their cheerful banter. I did not feel alone any more. I stood up in my cot and grinned at them, wickedly.

They grinned back, always delighted to see me, and began to play a game of "catch" which I loved, by throwing teddies and soft toys towards me. Of course I didn't manage to catch many, but those I did, I threw back to them, giggling all the while. I loved this game.

Sadly, my brothers, Jim and George soon got tired of this game and fell asleep. And my eldest brother, Richie was not home yet, but I was still wide awake. So after rattling the bars of my cot a few times, I wondered what to do.

It was still broad daylight outside, about 9pm with the late sun streaming through the window, so I toddled to the end of my cot and pulled back the curtain. My cot was right next to the window, so after collecting a few teddies, I dared to clamber up onto the windowsill and to stand there, looking down. I then managed to open the side-hinged window, having seen it done many times before, so I began to chuck all of my soft toys and teddies down into the garden below, watching in fascination to see where they landed.

My mum was downstairs in the kitchen at the time, making sandwiches for the next day's lunches. She could not possibly have known what was going on, as all was quiet in the boys' shared bedroom.

At that point, George woke up and rather groggily said, 'Get down, Lawrence - you might fall,' then promptly fell asleep again.

I was disappointed by my brothers' lack of interest, so much so, that I stepped further out of the window and stood precariously on the outside sill.

Realising I had no toys left to throw, I threw my empty bottle out and watched its descent as it got stuck in the bushes. But I was still wearing my "Batman" slippers, which I never liked to take off at bedtime, so my mum usually snuck in and took them off before she went to bed. These had plastic soles, and as I leaned forward to get a better look, my feet suddenly slipped and I fell - to go the same way as my toys and bottle had.

There was a tall, untrimmed privet hedge just below the bedroom window, and it was this that saved my life. All I can remember is falling through the scratchy bushes, a few feet at a time, turning this way and that, grabbing at branches here and there, which fortunately broke my fall, and of losing one slipper.

I somehow landed unhurt, stood up giddily and found the missing slipper which had landed a few feet away. Then I guess I must have cried a bit, then toddled round to the kitchen door to find my mum. She was still doing sandwiches with her back to me. As she heard me and spun around to see me walking in the back door holding one slipper and crying, she gasped in fright.

'What on earth–'

That was the first of my nine cat-lives. I had only one small scratch upon my head from my tangled descent through the bushes. Later, my mum ranted at my brothers for not taking care of me, and also at my dad for not screwing down the window latch which he kept meaning to do. He did it the very next day and that window was never opened again. As for my mum, she hadn't even realised that I was capable of climbing out of the cot, as she'd never seen me do it. But it wasn't really anyone else's fault. I guess I was just born a rebel.

Lawrence Palmer (b. 1975)

Four Half Crowns

I grew up in Collyhurst, an area of north Manchester. My parents were both stereotypical of the time, being hard working but unfortunately getting nowhere fast and, honest as the days were frugal and long. I suppose you could call us dirt poor because there was no shortage of grime and austerity in our lives as I grew up in the 1950s.

Simple games were played out in the cobbled streets around the identical endless rows of two up two down terraced houses. *Skipping, running, king of the castle, cowboys and Indians, hopscotch, football, big bad wolf* and many other games needing more imagination than money were played out from morning until late evening whilst my parents worked at a succession of low paid jobs.

I recall my mother or my 'Mam' working in the local *Chippy* peeling potatoes, then the *UCP tripe and Cow heel* shop as a counter assistant and, in later years she worked as a waitress at the *Kardoma* cafe in central Manchester, close to London Road railway station.

My Dad had been an unskilled labourer all his life working at the local gas works then at the *Mather and Platt* engineering works in Newton Heath. I remember when I was perhaps seven or eight years old my dad worked on gas lamp maintenance. He would be out most of the day and on into the late evenings, renewing the broken gas mantles and adjusting the regulators, then finally cleaning the four panes of glass with a grubby chamois leather before moving on to the next lamp.

My Dad travelled around the area on his old but trusty *Rudge* pedal cycle and carried an ex army shoulder bag full of the new gas mantles and the tools he needed for his job. He often returned late at night when he handed over the empty small white mantle boxes for me to play with. I made many castles and wobbly towers out of those throw away boxes as I played on the bare concrete floor in our back room before it was time for bed.

I received pocket money of two shillings from my Dad and sixpence from my Mam (half a crown in total, the equivalent of twelve and a half pence in today's money) that usually went on three penny (thrupence) lucky bags or other sweets. The *lucky* bags contained a small plastic toy and two to three pieces of sugary confectionery of dubious quality!

I decided at one stage to build my own 'OO' *Hornby* railway layout in sections and proceeded to buy one piece of track a week until I had enough for a three foot circle of track. I had to save up for a couple of weeks more before I managed to buy a locomotive, a little blue 0-4-0 tank loco called *Nellie*!

I also needed a power source so purchased three 4.5 volt 'Bell' batteries. I couldn't afford the speed controller that fitted on top of the batteries so got my Dad to wire the batteries up to the track... but it didn't work! So my Dad put the whole lot in a box and took the layout and me down to the shop to solve the mystery. I often wonder what the shopkeeper thought of my Dads wiring capabilities! He never said, but proceeded to sell my dad the correct *Meccano* controller and the plug in connector for the track (I had mistakenly bought an isolator track that would never have been able to provide the twelve volts to the loco!).

After we had finally got it all working, a mate, (Johnny Gibson) decided he would have a railway layout too, although he didn't have to save up like I did and got the money for the whole list of parts in one go. I knew the system now and informed him he needed a bell battery controller. A young lady assistant served us instead of the usual shopkeeper, and when we got home found to our delight that the box contained three controllers!

So we now had two each! My Dad soon spotted the extra controller though and marched me round to my mates, then to the model shop where we had to return the other two!

As well as working his regular day job my Dad carried out little repair jobs around our streets, his speciality being to repair broken windows. Although he never knew it, some of his regular extra income was down to me, as I was a crack shot with a catapult! I doubt my Dad would have appreciated the financial or ironical side of the arrangement and I would probably have ended up with a good hiding!

My Dad had made himself a two wheeled handcart to transport his tools and panes of glass around the area, which came in handy one day when someone from the *'richer'* Victorian terrace houses about a quarter of a mile away, had given him a giant wooden wardrobe to dispose of. I steadied the huge bulk of the wardrobe on the handcart as my Dad struggled and sweated with the precarious load the one road, two streets and one croft we needed to negotiate to get to our house.

When we had finally managed to get the wardrobe upstairs to the front bedroom my Dad had gone out to the shops for his regular order of pipe tobacco and left me alone to examine our latest acquisition. I convinced myself that this dark grainy wood, glossy finished wardrobe was the actual one that contained the magic secret back panel that would enable me to travel to Narnia as in the book, The Lion, The Witch and The Wardrobe, to slay the evil witch! The lower section of the wardrobe contained a huge single drawer that had been tied with old string whilst in transit. I feverishly undid the knotted, mangled string and hauled out the heavy drawer... looking inside the huge chasm I noticed a small brown envelope... I picked it up... something jingled... Then I emptied the envelope out on the bed... Four half crowns fell out! We were rich! I quickly worked out that I could purchase forty lucky bags! I ran down the stairs with my colossal monetary find straight into my Dad, who was just coming back through the front door. I blurted out about the envelope and the four half crowns. My Dad needed no time to ponder what to do with our sudden wealth as he took me by the arm straight back to the Victorian terrace house, up the flight of five steps, and knocked on the door.

I can relate the events clear as day that unfolded over the next two minutes. The door opened and my Dad said, 'Yes' to which the house owner replied, 'We have no Bananas!' The sickly humour was wasted on me as I was more interested in the half crowns. My Dad patted my head as he quickly explained about me finding the four half crowns in the drawer, whereupon the house owner quickly snatched the envelope out of my Dads hand, and then proceeded to slam the door shut in our faces! Not so much as a thank you, no appreciation of his honesty, nothing.

I was crestfallen to say the least as we walked back to our house in silence, my Dad said nothing with his head slightly bowed as he moved along with a slightly shuffling gait.

It wasn't until much later in life that I reflected about that day, and what my Dad had possibly been feeling, as he never mentioned the incident to me again. Did he feel proud that he had '*done the right thing*' and taken the money back, or did he feel stupid and embarrassed in front of his young son at the outcome? I will never know, as my dad passed away in September of 1980.

One thing I do know is that my Dads honesty on that day has always stayed with me and made me the person I am today.

I work at many houses in my job and pride myself on the fact that I am trusted to come and go and to hold the keys of their property when they are away. I value that trust above all else, knowing that I inherited my Dads total honesty; an honesty that shines out from its humble roots, and lives on in his proud son to this day.

God bless you Dad, RIP.

Dave Clarke b.1951

54

Gary the Archer

When I was about nine years old, Mum had to go into hospital, so Nan and Granddad came round to look after us. They brought my two sisters and me a present each. I think it was dolls for them; but my present was a cool bow and arrow, which fortunately (as it turned out), was tipped with a rubber suction pad and therefore not lethal. I had a target board that I placed at the top of the stairs on a door. From the bottom of the stairs I practised shooting my arrow for an hour or so and became quite a good shot. I'd read all the usual advice and info about eyeing the target and letting your brain take over. I guessed I was a natural 'Robin Hood'.

But then I got bored and I took my bow and arrow outside. I was wondering what to have as my new target, so tried aiming at a few birds, but they were too quick for me and all escaped easily. Then I shot a few heads off my dad's sunflowers, which I knew would not go down well. Next I saw Jamie, the boy next door in his garden. I asked him if he wanted to play. He said 'no' as he had to do some weeding jobs for his dad, then turned his back to me.

I felt a bit disgruntled by this time. It was okay for my sisters; they were busily engaged playing with their daft dollies. So why did I have to be an outcast with no-one to play with? I took aim, shot the arrow and hit Jamie in the back of the head, which knocked him out cold. I must admit that I panicked at the sight of him lying there unconscious, and ran back into the house to hide in my bedroom.

As it turned out, Jamie wasn't concussed or anything serious – he'd simply been knocked out. But I had my bow and arrow confiscated and had to go and apologise to him once they had arrived back from the hospital. I guess I wasn't such a great 'Robin Hood' after all.

When I was fifteen years old we went on a fortnight's family camping holiday in Plymouth, which I had really looked forward to. Plymouth is a beautiful city with lots of great beaches and nearby attractions.

After sampling most of these delights, and on about the fourth evening we all got ready to go up to the social club on site. We spent a very pleasant evening there with loads of entertainment for kids and grown-ups alike. But then as we came out we noticed that the wind was high and the rain was torrential. As we made our way back to our tent, we saw other people struggling to secure their tents in the bad weather. When we arrived back at our tent we decided that it would be best to sleep in the car rather than in the tent. We first checked that the tent was secure, then made our way back to the car.

While in the car, trying to sleep, you could feel the vehicle move and rock in the high wind, which was really scary, but eventually we slept. When we awoke in the morning, the wind had calmed down and it had stopped raining. However, when we got out of the car, we saw that our tent was still secured down and OK, but there were at least twenty tents at the bottom of the hill in pieces.

So I guess we did something right.

Gary Burne (b. 1970)

Goldfish Pond

My sister and I were walking through a small park in Washington DC. It wasn't much more than a block square and a lovely shortcut on our walk home from wherever we wandered. In the 40s children could more safely explore their neighborhoods than they can now, and we went walking around our area just about every day. I was six years old, and Iris, my sister, was four. It was winter, and we were wearing heavy wool coats.

In this park was a goldfish pond. It was rather formal with a concrete ledge all around its rectangular space so that visitors could sit and watch the fish. The bottom was tiled, and as I remember it, there wasn't much in the way of vegetation. It was also rather large—probably twenty by ten feet, although when I revisit places in my adult years, I'm always surprised at how small things really were.

Instead of sitting on the ledge, though, both of us walked on it like we were doing a tightrope act—arms extended to keep our balance. Iris loved the water, and even in her later years, she was drawn to the beach and loved to swim. It showed up early in her life on this day. She thought it would be fun to grab a fish, so when she leaned over to do it, she lost her balance and fell into the water. I can still see her green coat floating on the top of the water and her blonde hair spread out upon it as well. Her face was in the water, and for long seconds she didn't seem to move at all. I quickly grabbed the bottom of her coat before she floated too far away and pulled her to the shallower side where she stood up, dripping wet and crying, of course. All I could think of was how I'd get blamed if anything happened to her. I was always in charge and responsible.

As we were hurrying home, a policeman crossed our path and expressed horror at Iris's wet condition in such cold weather. He offered to drive us home, but being only a block away from our house, I assured him we were almost there. I was terrified over this incident, but Iris was babbling all the way home about how she opened her eyes under the water and watched the fish swim all around her; for her it was an adventure!

It's amazing how we remember things.

Carole Devine (b. 1939)

The Guider and the Martini Henry!

There were very few cars around or much traffic of any description when I was a lad growing up in the Collyhurst area of north Manchester. We never aspired to car ownership anyway and the trusty bus or regular steam train journeys were the norm.

One item that provided the means to ready, basic transport however for the young motor-less entrepreneur was a ready supply of old pram wheels that were often discarded around the area. I was also extremely fortunate in that my Dad possessed a reasonable wood-working tool kit with the addition of a good stock of nails, screws and carriage bolts of varying lengths.

Having found two good pieces of three quarter inch thick timber and a wooden soft drinks box, I set to work with youthful enthusiasm. Ten minutes engrossed into the project and I became aware that the back door was being violently pounded on by a distraught neighbour complaining that my hammering was disturbing his sleep after working the night shift. He informed me that he would pay for the job as long as I kept quiet! I missed my chance though as I wasn't that savvy when it came to matters of a financial nature. There must have been an easy couple of bob pick- up there somewhere, I later mused!

Not to be outdone by this sudden interruption, I loaded all my parts and tools onto the wood planks tied to the wheel axles and continued with the construction two streets away!

My dad was none too pleased at my neighbour's outburst when I later informed him of what had happened, as he too often worked nights. He went round to confront the man and a heated exchange took place. I don't know exactly what was said but my dad told me to carry on with whatever it was I was making, and to let him know if anyone came round again complaining. No one ever did and I soon finished my project. Our local dialect referred to these contraptions as 'guiders', but there were many names including soap box or billy carts.

I was very pleased with my finished cart as it had a carpet covered seat with a hinged lid fashioned from the drinks box, rope and foot operated steering, a parking plus lever operated hand brake. Not bad workmanship for a nine year old!

I had cleverly removed some of the partitioning in the box seat leaving three sections for plastic drinks containers of water or fizzy drinks and a couple of tools. The larger section was used to store my overcoat and my lunch which usually consisted of two rounds of white bread plastered in margarine topped off with a good mound of granulated sugar! Instant energy food for a young explorer!

My cart became the object of instant envy from the local urchins who lacked the brains or the temperament to build one for them-selves. They would sometimes lie in wait and pelt me with sods of grass or stones as I smugly cruised past.

I started to venture further and further afield with my guider to avoid these green-eyed monsters, one of my favourite near places however was Queens Park, situated about a quarter of a mile away from where I lived. The park contained two areas of woodland known locally as 'the big valley and the little valley'. Towards the back of the big valley a levelled but vastly overgrown area contained a large, long forgotten, weed infested graveyard. This was one of my favourite 'haunts', pun intended! One day as I was scything my way through the vine choked undergrowth, there suddenly appeared in front of me a plain red brick and concrete derelict building that resembled one of the multitudes of WW11 air raid shelters that littered the area. I pulled away the weeds and spindly bush growth that half covered the entrance and peered inside... Pitch black and smelling very musty. I thrust my hand in my pocket and retrieved one of my other great inventions... A home-made matchbox torch! (A simple bulb wired to a small battery with a crude but effective switch made from a bent piece of tin, housed neatly in the box).

Inside the 'shelter', the dirt floor was littered with bits of rotted wood and tin cans. The ground was soft to walk on and after I had taken five or six steps inside I had, like all little boys, the sudden urge to dig in the dirt! I set to work with one of the tin cans and soon unearthed a lump of heavy pipe. I carried it outside to inspect my find in daylight to discover to my delight that I had unearthed a gun! The gun was in a very sorry state indeed with advanced corrosion on the barrel and lock mechanism, it had also been shortened by the removal of half the stock, suggesting a dark and somewhat chequered history.

After I returned home I set to with a scraper and scrubbing brush to reveal a Martini Henry carbine rifle, the type issued to cavalry or training cadets. The rifle of .577 inch calibre was manufactured mainly by the Royal Small Arms Factory, Enfield, from 1871 to 1888 and became the standard issue of the British army. (I knew nothing of this at the time of course and researched my find in later years). A good illustration of the rifle (not the carbine version) in action can be found in the film 'Zulu' made in 1964.

Scrubbed and scraped clean the carbine looked fairly presentable although it would not have been capable of firing a shot in anger ever again as the lock mechanism had corroded and seized solid; it was, however, of a good manageable size and weight and a trusty accompaniment to a young, intrepid explorer.

I fixed the carbine in a loose fashion to the side of my guider with a couple of leather straps 'borrowed' from my sister's roller skates that she no longer used anyway.

I sometimes think back to those long hot summers (and they truly were!) when I would take my guider, Martini Henry carbine and sugar butties exploring the overgrown wastelands, bombed out houses and factories that were still in abundance around Manchester even into the late 1960s.

The guider was eventually stolen from our back yard along with the Martini Henry after I had enjoyed them both for a couple of wonderful summers. I was not particularly put out at the time though as I had just started a new project. I had swapped some toys for a red bicycle or more accurately, a frame, two wheels, a pair of handlebars and a seat loosely bolted to the frame at a ridiculous angle. The first time I rode it I nearly broke my ankles as it was fitted with a fixed gear arrangement.

A friend of mine knew someone that was selling his stock of bicycle spares, so we both went round to see what he had. For my project I managed to buy both of the complete brake assemblies, an almost new crank, chain and free-wheeling sprocket, plus lots of other bits for just two shillings (10p). This lad was a lot older than us and informed us that he was selling his push bike stuff as he was saving up for a deposit to buy a motorbike on his sixteenth birthday just four weeks away.

Sadly, he never made it... two weeks later he was killed while riding pillion on his mate's motorbike.

I managed to complete the construction of my bicycle and we went on to cover many miles and to have lots of great adventures together. The finished bike was a far cry from the original item with lots of chrome fittings on the red frame with blue mudguards and a matching saddlebag that often housed my bottle of pop and sugar butties. I owned this bike for four years before I started work, I then sold it to buy a brand new five speed racing model, a Dawes Dalesman.

Dave Clarke born 1951

Happy Days – NOT!

My childhood was somewhat 'different' to say the least, with Mum and I always in bed before Dad got home at pub chucking-out time. If there was no-one around for him to thump or argue with when he got in, he generally went fairly quickly to sleep. However, I couldn't do that until I had heard the crescendo of the slow thudding of his steps up the stairs followed by at least five minutes of silence or, better still, his stentorian snoring. God knows how Mum slept through that, but I guess even if it woke her there was a certain sense of relief in knowing that, at least for tonight, there would be no fisticuffs.

I recall one night when I was about twelve. We had an old banger of a car parked in the back yard and Dad eventually got it going, as they had decided, on one of their rare truce-nights, to have a night out together. It had no petrol in it however, so I was despatched to take a petrol can to a garage up the road and bring back a gallon of fuel to get it started. I did as I was bid and managed to spill some over my legs as I filled the can.

When I returned, I set behind the sofa as we had an open coal fire at the time, and I had no desire to be suddenly engulfed in flames. My dad laughed and said 'don't be daft, it'll have evaporated by now,' but he didn't know the full reason for my fear. The petrol was the least of my worries as I knew that even as they were getting ready to go out, they wouldn't return home together. This also meant that both Mum and I would, by dint of them going out together, still be around when he got home soused. In those days, I'm not even sure that the law about drink-driving existed and even if it had, I doubt that it would have stopped Dad. He was a long-distance lorry driver and used his sixteen-wheel articulated lorry as if it were a company car at night, driving it down to the pub and home again afterwards. I imagine that driving a car drunk was probably small potatoes to him.

I stayed home alone, watching telly and then, as it got later and all the TV stations closed down, switching on the old Bush battery-driven transistor radio to tune in to the only through-the-night entertainment there was at that time: Radio Luxembourg on 208 metres medium-wave. They played pop music all through the night but the signal would irritatingly ebb and flow as if it were being transmitted from a rotating radar mast. Eventually, tiredness got the better of me and I gave up my vigil and went to bed, falling relatively quickly to sleep.

I was awoken by a knock on the door some time later – I have no idea what time – and it was Dad *on his own*. My worst fears had come true and my dad was only capable of an incoherent mumbling to my repeated question of 'Where's Mum? Where's Mum?'

He stomped off upstairs and I, now wide awake, once again took up my Luxembourg-accompanied vigil. It seems that I waited an age and still no mum and once more my eyelids began to droop, so I was forced to go back to bed resolving to find out what happened from Dad tomorrow.

Some time in the middle of the night I was slowly roused from a fairly deep sleep, thinking I was still partly dreaming, as I could hear the clomp-clomp-clomp of footsteps up and down the entry that ran front-to-back between us and next door with alternated hammering on the front and back doors. As I came fully awake, I could also hear some muffled sobs at the same time and I came round immediately when I realised it was Mum. I went downstairs and let her in – Dad had put the latch on before going to bed so her key wouldn't work and she couldn't get in. I was wearing only a vest and was freezing, it being god-knows-what-time in the middle of the night, and Mum wouldn't tell me what had happened and just told me to go back to bed, so I did. At least if they were going to argue some more it wouldn't be until tomorrow when Dad had slept it off, and he was much less violent when sober.

I had to go to school the following day so if there was an ensuing argument, I wasn't witness to it for once. I later found out that they had begun arguing in the car on the way home and Dad had abruptly stopped the car and forced Mum to get out about five miles from home then drove off without her. There were no 24-hour taxi services then, so she had no alternative but to walk home.

At least one good thing (from my point of view) came out of it: they never did go out again together and Mum wouldn't get in the car again at any time, night or day.

Jim Ollerhead (b.1955)

Hemlock

I skipped out of the school gate, quite happily, clutching my latest masterpiece – a drawing to show Mum. Then I stopped in sudden bewilderment, for Mum's clapped-out old Mini was nowhere to be seen.

What could have happened? Mum always met me from school, even though I was twelve years old and only lived around the corner. There was no real need for her to pick me up, but she always did, and I'd grown to expect it. Although I did not realise it at the time, I guess I was a bit spoilt.

I walked home, crossly. It took only ten minutes, or so. I marched through the front door, and slammed it rather more loudly than was necessary. Mum was not in the kitchen, as expected, so I stormed into the front room. There I halted my tirade in shock.

Mum was there; but so was a stranger. He was old – at least thirty-five, and was sitting close to Mum on the settee. There were half-empty glasses of wine on the coffee table before them. Even worse, this man had his arm around Mum's shoulder, and she looked all flushed and giggly – not at all her usual self.

'Hello, Hannah,' Mum said, 'sorry I didn't meet you from school – I thought you might like to walk home with your friends for a change.'

I think I scowled. I didn't have any friends - didn't want any. The other kids thought I was much too clever for them. There was only me and Mum since Dad had run off with another woman, and that was just the way I liked it. I hated men anyway.

'I want you to meet David,' Mum said, amicably. 'He's a dear friend of mine.'

David turned and extended his hand. 'Hello Hannah,' he said, gently, 'I am pleased to meet you – you are almost as pretty as your mother.'

I almost flounced like a spoiled toddler, but just remembered to keep my dignity. I ignored the proffered hand, pretending not to have noticed it. 'Hello,' I said curtly. 'I'm hungry!' I then announced to Mum.

'There's plenty of left-over casserole in the kitchen,' Mum said. 'You only have to pop it in the microwave for a few minutes.'

'Okay,' I said. David was putting his head close to Mum's again. I fled from the room in disgust.

I looked at the half-congealed casserole – it would have been okay – Mum was a good cook; but then I caught a snatch of their conversation from the front room. Mum was saying, 'She'll get used to the idea. Give her time...' Suddenly I didn't feel hungry any more. I flew upstairs to my bedroom and flung myself on the bed. Then I remembered the special drawing which I'd been going to show Mum, the one I'd got an A plus for. I retrieved it from my school-bag and tore it up into little pieces which I threw all over the floor. Then I collapsed, once more, sobbing on the bed. David was going to ruin my life, I just knew it.

I hated him already.

Several weeks passed and it was almost Easter time. David was still seeing Mum and I still hated him, but at least he hadn't moved in or anything awful like that. They went out together once a week and as he worked evening shift, David would come round for a late supper twice a week, usually after I'd gone to bed which suited me fine, as I hardly ever saw him. But I knew they were only waiting for me to accept David before they went and got married, or something equally stupid. I was determined not to let this happen. I must have been a right selfish little cow back then, because I didn't even consider how much happier Mum looked since meeting David. I only thought about Me.

Then one afternoon while I was doing homework in my room, I formed a brilliant plan to get rid of David. We'd been learning about poisonous plants in Biology and for homework I had to draw one. After looking in the text book for pictures, I'd decided on poison hemlock. I loved drawing and wasn't bad at it. I recognised this plant at once, as I admired the huge palmate leaves and creamy-white umbelliferous flowers. Then I greatly enjoyed drawing it in detail, even mixing up just the right shade of blackish-green to colour the leaves. As I worked, I began to think of the teacher's words in the lesson, 'Poison hemlock is the deadliest known poison plant that is native to Britain. Cattle and sheep often die from accidentally eating it.'

I paused with my brush in mid air. David would be coming for his late supper tonight. Mum was even now making our (and his) favourite curried casserole. She always put his portion aside in a separate dish, for him to eat later. Did I really dare?

It was still daylight until about 6pm at that time of year and I knew exactly where some poison hemlock was growing on nearby wasteland. I told Mum I was just nipping out to the library to look something up for my homework.

She said, 'All right dear, but be quick – dinner will be ready in half an hour.' never suspecting my evil intention.

I quickly reached the wasteland and was back in twenty minutes with two huge hemlock leaves safely stowed in my pocket.

After dinner, I told Mum that I'd do the washing-up while she went to watch her favourite soap. She looked a bit surprised at this offer, as I wasn't usually so helpful. I explained that I'd had really easy homework, especially after checking at the library, and had flown through it.

'You are such a good girl,' she said, smiling sweetly, which made me feel guilty as hell.

Now for the deadly deed. I first stacked the dishes in a sink full of hot sudsy water to let them soak. David's dinner was in a small covered dish on top of the cooker. I rinsed off the hemlock leaves, then chopped them very finely on the bread board, until they resembled mint sauce or fresh herbs. Then I stirred them into the casserole. I remembered to add some more turmeric in case the curry looked too greenish, and then some more curry powder to disguise any unpleasant taste, then I washed up all the utensils I'd used along with the other dishes.

At ten o'clock, I said goodnight to Mum and went off to bed. David would arrive about eleven to meet his fate. Not unnaturally, I had some difficulty getting to sleep.

But I must've dropped off in the end, because I was suddenly woken up by the phone ringing, and ringing... Thinking Mum must have gone to sleep early, I finally went downstairs to answer it.

It was Mum. 'Hello, Hannah,' she said. 'I'm sorry I had to rush off and leave you. I'm at the hospital.'

I suddenly remembered what I'd done with a spasm of guilt. *Had it happened already? Was David dead?* 'What's wrong Mum?' I managed to mumble.

'It's David,' she informed. 'He couldn't make it tonight as he had an accident at work and caught his fingers in machinery. He's OK. They've patched him up and are just keeping him in overnight for observation. I'll be getting a taxi home, so could you put that leftover curry in the oven please, dear. I'll eat it for supper myself to save wasting it.'

I guess she always wondered why I slammed the phone down and fled to the kitchen, but all I could think of as I disposed of the poisoned food was:

Thank God she phoned...

Anonymous (b.1972)

Hens Crowing Sadly

I grew up with three brothers and one sister and once, when we kids were quite young, my mum and step-dad purchased six ex-battery hens that were considered to be too old for rapid egg production. These were intended as pets for us children and to live out their retirement in peace (and to save them from the pot), although they still laid beautiful large double-yolked eggs.

These feathery friends were housed in a converted shed with lots of hay and perches – plus they had the full run of a massive wild garden of just grass. It was a joy to see them the first time they were let loose. I guess they'd never seen grass before – and they loved it. I immediately adopted the weakest and feeblest one which seemed to be lowest in the pecking order. I called her 'Georgie' (after me) and always looked out for her when she was bullied by the others.

Georgie often tried to sneak into the kitchen and roost on the work surface. She looked quite at home and comfortable there; but of course my mum couldn't allow this for hygienic reasons, so I had to pick her up and take her back to the chicken run every time.

We fed them mostly on the usual chicken feed from the pet shop, and they scratched up loads of worms themselves, which must've been a real treat for them. However during cold weather, my mum made them potato mash, mixed with crushed eggshells and various vegetable peelings which she boiled up specially. They seemed to love this too.

After a time, my step-dad purchased a young cockerel, simply because he was beautiful - all red, green and gold, a real Rhode Island Red - and obviously the old chickadees after the initial pecking order ritual, were dead chuffed with him and seemed happier than ever.

We kids loved 'em. We would squabble over who was going to feed the chickens or collect the eggs, until my mum drew up a rota - and every morning one would unlock the shed to release the hens. Every evening, the chickens would return to the shed of their own accord, seeming to know by instinct that this was "home".

Then came the terrible night when the child whose turn it was forgot to lock the shed. And it wasn't me.

The next morning, the scene of devastation was grim indeed. Only one hen was missing, but all the others lay dead and mutilated. Charlie, the gorgeous cockerel had a massive chunk bitten out of his green-feathered throat. He was furthest away from the shed and had obviously given chase, trying to protect his family. The other hens were just strewn around in various bloodied heaps – including Georgie.

I cried for Georgie. We all cried for the dear chickens. We knew it was a fox, even without seeing the tuft of red fur in Charlie's beak. How could Mum then explain to her sobbing children that foxes are just seeking food the same as any other animal? So why kill seven, then take only one?

No, I don't condone the cruelty of fox-hunting, but I still think that red, gold and green feathers look better on a chicken than in a fox's gob!

George Palmer (b.1972)

It was a Great Laugh

I was born in Caversham, Reading, Berkshire. We moved to Tilehurst when I was three years old. I can remember going out to play to meet my new friends.

A little boy came up to me and said, 'What's your name?' Because my name is Gloria, I couldn't even pronounce it at all. I had to take him to my mum to ask her what my name was.

I went to Grovelands Primary School, which was just down the road from my house. I learned to swim when I was five, as we were very lucky to have our own swimming pool at school. I grew up with four brothers, so I ended up being a right little tomboy. We used to go scrumping over the allotments behind our street; we would come back with armfuls of rhubarb, goosegogs, apples and all sorts.

My mum used to say, 'And where did you get these from?'

We used to reply, 'A sweet little man gave us them from his allotment.' But that, of course, was not true; he used to chase us off with a gun.

We had an old battle-axe who lived on the corner. She used to come and shout at us all the time (she didn't like kids at all), so when it was dark we used to go and fall into her hedge, which she had all the way round her garden. It ended up looking like a zig-zag instead of a pristine, neat border. I think she knew who the culprits were but could never prove it.

I went to Wilson Secondary School. I had two best friends. We were always together; we had great fun. It was the time when mini-skirts were in fashion and boy, did we wear them short!

We were once caught smoking in the toilets and had to go and see the Headmistress, Mrs Prior. She was scary; we had the ruler rapped on our knuckles (boy that hurt) and we were put on the smokers' list. I was always in trouble for talking or laughing and would spend most lessons standing outside the classroom. The teachers would always come past me and say, 'And what are you out here for again Bark?' That was my maiden name.

When we had P.E in the hall, we would always be mucking about; we used to sit on the floor and deliberately fart (it certainly echoed around the hall) and we would be in trouble yet again.

But all in all, we turned out to be quite reasonably well-adjusted people and I don't think all that messing about did us any harm.

We just had fun.

Gloria Clark (b.1953)

Julie's Time Out

Once, when I was about nine years old, I told Mum I did not feel very well and needed the day off school. Like most mums in those days, she was prepared to give me the benefit of the doubt, especially as I didn't malinger very often.

Lindsey, my sister, who was two years older, did not want to leave me for the day, so Mum agreed to let us both have time off school.

We spent the whole day playing astronauts which involved us jumping around our shared bedroom and pretending we were at zero gravity. We enacted various imaginary missions throughout the day, but every time we heard Mum's footsteps on the stairs, I would dive back into bed and Lindsey would have a book on standby to be reading to me, while I lay back against the pillow, looking all hot and bothered.

I don't think we were ever proven guilty but I'm sure Mum had her doubts about how unwell I really was. Parents are not so naïve as we imagine when we're young.

Julie's Student Exchange

When I was fourteen years old, I went to Germany on a student exchange. I stayed with Christiana and her lovely family who were very welcoming, even though I didn't speak much German at the time.

I stayed with them for two weeks and every morning my exchange partner's mum laid out a wonderful breakfast of breads, hams, cheese and suchlike. At the time I was vegetarian and didn't like cheese, so could only eat the bread, which did not taste quite the same as Asda's own white bread at home. Funny, I never thought I was a finicky eater before, but this holiday proved to me that it's what you're used to that counts.

I ended up over the next fourteen days losing quite a bit of weight - nearly a stone.

On my last morning with Christiana's family I was in the kitchen with her when she opened a cupboard and I saw a box of Coco Pops. I mentioned to her that they were my favourite breakfast cereal. She then explained to me that the family did normally just help themselves to cereal or toast in the mornings, but as I was a guest, her mum had made a special effort and laid out the full traditional German breakfast for me.

Christiana's kind mum had not realised that I would have preferred to have toast and cereal, as I was unable to eat most of her traditional breakfast each morning. So much for intercontinental communication! I resolved to improve my German after that, as Christiana's English put mine to shame.

My mum met me at the airport and looked aghast when she saw the new sylph-like me. 'What have they done to you?' she asked.

Julie Morris (b.1981)

I Remember Ken Green

Ken Green was... an evacuee. He had heard bombs fall, collected shrapnel and had seen an enemy plane shot down. To the rest of us at the Wigston Magna National School he seemed to have led a charmed and adventurous life.

My name is Terry and I'd better begin at the beginning. I was aged eight and the year was 1941. Far away from bombs and the war, I lived in Wigston Leicestershire.

Ken was one of a group of recently arrived evacuees from London. He was billeted near to where I lived, with a family that had two girls, Sheila and Betty, and their mother and father. Ken was not impressed by the girls, who were slightly older than he was, or by their authoritarian father.

Ken's mother had remained in London doing war work and his father was a soldier stationed in the North of Africa. The excitement on Ken's face was a joy to see when he received a distinctive red and blue striped airmail letter from his father. He carried it round for days peeking at it often, sometimes even in class. The teachers were very understanding and didn't make an issue of it; besides on those days his behaviour was much less mischievous.

Ken and I became friends; very good friends and we had lots of fun. We got into all sorts of mischief together, usually of Ken's making.

For instance, one day when returning to school after we'd been home for our lunch Ken suggested we went via the allotments. Besides the usual wartime Dig for Victory vegetables: carrots, peas, beans, onions, potatoes etc, the allotments also had fruit trees. In the sunshine the red apples on the tree looked tempting, so we climbed the tree and took a few apples. An old man at the other end of the allotments waved his stick and shouted at us, nothing new there—we'd heard all those swear words before! As we scrambled down from the tree we put our tongues out at him and ran away.

Each munching on an apple, we made our way back to school, trying to think of excuses to explain our lateness. We rounded the last corner and in front of us was a large, red-faced, very angry man.

"Where do you think you're going? You've been bothering my father, you little b*****s," he roared. "When I catch you you'll get a clip round the ears."

We took one look at his clenched hands, turned and glanced at each other; Ken winked—then we both ran like stink in opposite directions. We didn't go to school that afternoon and—not having sick notes next morning—got caned by the headmaster for playing truant!

Another day as we walked past the local baker's on the way home for lunch the smell of freshly baked bread was fantastic and Ken suggested we called in. The various types of bread on show looked very appealing, so we pooled our few coins and bought a cottage loaf. Once outside the shop it was quickly pulled apart and shared. The warm and crusty bread tasted out of this world; but of course on reaching our respective homes, neither of us had any appetite for any lunch!

One of our regular play areas was on the railway embankment. In one or two places tracks leading to farmers' fields crossed over the railway. Where each of these unmade roads crossed the lines it had its own bridge, just wide enough for horse and cart or tractor and trailer. The sidewalls of these bridges were of steel with a narrow parapet running along the outside to deflect the train smoke away from the metalwork. For a dare, we'd climb over the outside of the bridge and walk along the parapet with the bridge's steel wall to one side of us and nothing on the other, except the rails 30 feet (10m) below. It was of course extremely dangerous and very exciting. If a train came along, being on the parapet over the line that the train was on was not the best place to be, you got covered in hot smoke and steam—no diesels in those days.

Another railway dare, when the small stream that crossed underneath the railway was not too full, was to crawl along the circular 4 foot (1½m) diameter tunnel that ran under the embankment. That dare wasn't too bad—if you didn't mind the wet and slime if your feet slipped off the sides where you'd had to wedge them to keep out of the water! If a train came before you got out the other end, all sorts of creeping things including spiders would fall on you as the vibrations from the train shook the tunnel. There was only one girl that we knew who dared to do it.

Ken had a lively imagination, he'd tell stories which although far fetched, I half believed. For instance he said that in London, he'd used his grandfather's First World War pistol to capture a German pilot who'd parachuted from a plane that had been shot down.

Another time he told us that where he lived, there was a mad inventor who made very large models of planes like Spitfires and Hurricanes that you could actually sit in. During one raid on London, Ken said that he'd actually flown one of these and had shot down two German bombers. Ken also told us the inventor had a small submarine that he'd been in.

It was only years later with hindsight, did I realise that Ken's adventures always followed a conversation we'd had when thinking out loud "Wouldn't it be good if there was a plane we could fly?" "Wouldn't it be good if there was a submarine we could use in the quarry?"

Poor lonely Ken, far away from his familiar home in the big city; two unsympathetic foster sisters for company, his mother working in London, and his father in danger as a soldier fighting the Germans in the desert. Ken needed a friend who'd take notice of him—and I was the very gullible child who filled that need.

Ken returned to London before the war ended and I went on to grammar school after passing the 11 plus. I sometimes think of those times at Wigston Magna National School and wonder what Ken Green is doing now and if he ever thinks of his school days in Leicestershire.

N.B. *The story is true but names have been changed as some of the people are still alive.*

Anonymous b.1935

Kindness and Courage

I will never forget the day I came home from primary school and found a stranger in our home – a dirty, ragged old man who stank to high heaven and who lunched at our table with my mother.

The scene shocked my young mind. What was happening here? Where did this person come from? Who was he that he should be sitting at our kitchen table in the middle of the day?

My mother rose from the table without fuss or ceremony and approached me as I stood gaping from the hallway. She helped me off with my raincoat, and I put my schoolbag on a hook. Pointing to the shadowy figure sitting in the kitchen, silhouetted against the window, his grey hair wild and unkempt, she told me who he was.

'Son, this is Mr Henderson, and he is having lunch with us today.'

I froze at the sight of the old man, sitting there in rags like a character out of Dickensian London, the odour from his body so vile I wanted to race to the toilet and retch. He staggered to his feet when my mother introduced him.

'How do you do, son. Your mother speaks fondly of you.'

I managed to grin at the visitor then looked up at my mother, hoping for further information, but none was forthcoming.

He slumped into his chair again and continued with his meal, scrambled eggs, toast, tomatoes, and a pot of tea. He seemed quite at ease.

My mother joined him, and he half-rose as she approached.

'Wash your hands and come and sit down,' she told me.

After a quick rinse under the tap behind my mother's back, I positioned myself at the table next to her. I dared not look at the stranger, fearing he might draw me into conversation and I would find myself tongue-tied.

'Tell me, John,' said my mother to the ragged creature at the other side of the table, 'what was it like at Monte Casino – apart from being dreadful?'

His eyes glazed over. He stopped chewing for a moment and laid his knife and fork at the sides of his plate.

'It was a living nightmare,' he croaked.

'I'm sure.'

'It was something no-one should have to go through.'

My mother glanced at me and continued: 'And... Was it there that you had your accident, John?'

He picked up his knife and fork again. They seemed to hover in mid-air as he contemplated my mother's question.

'Gangrene set in on the way home, you see, and they had to...' He threw a concerned glance at me. 'They had to take the legs off in a hospital in Southampton.'

A silence fell over us. I was appalled to think that he didn't have any legs. So how did he stand and walk, I wondered.

'You've managed to get around quite a bit, despite your difficulties, John,' my mother said at last with a measure of mirth lacing her words.

'Aye, Jean,'the legs haven't stopped me, or rather the lack of them. But they caused a lot of heartache in the personal sense. 'You see, my wife left me when I came back home. She didn't want a husband without legs. She just couldn't live with the shame. And I don't really blame her.'

'For better or worse,' my mother offered. 'Isn't that part of the marriage vows?'

'Aye, Jean, it's part of the marriage vows, but she couldn't face the idea, me having no legs and hobbling around for the rest of my life. Like I said, I don't blame her – but I miss her.'

I looked at the man now as I munched on my toast and marmalade. He seemed so isolated and lonely at the end of the table, cut off from us and everyone else, as he pondered his memories.

'I don't feel sorry for myself, you understand.'

'Of course not, John. I can see that.'

He picked up a napkin and dabbed his mouth with a hard, dirt-engrained, claw-like hand. 'I'd better be getting back to Sutton House,' he said, his face suddenly wistful.

'Is that the place you mentioned earlier, for the homeless?'

'It is, Jean. At least it's a roof over my head at night, but I wouldn't recommend it otherwise. It's a wild sort of place, full of drunks, and fights are a hair's breadth away most of the time. You rarely get more than a couple of hours' sleep.'

'Where is your wife now, John?' Mum voiced the question that I'd been dying to ask.

'Ireland, I believe. She took up with a Cork man, I heard, and moved to Ireland a few months after leaving me.'

'And what about your children?'

'No, we didn't have any children. We planned to at first, but it never happened. Maybe that's for the best.'

John reached for his crutches, which lay on the floor by the window, and hauled himself upright. My mother moved to help him, but he managed to refuse her help without giving offence.

'How far is it to this Sutton House?' she asked.

'About two miles. I can walk through the park and along the river. It's a fine walk on a sunny afternoon.'

My mother considered his words then said to me, 'Son, you walk with Mr Henderson to Main Street and see that he gets to the park all right.'

'There's no need...'

'It's okay, John. The little fella can get me some milk and bread on the way back.'

The three of us stood at the front door, and my mother leaned over and embraced the wretch before her. She kissed his forehead and slipped some wrapped sandwiches in his tattered overcoat pockets.

'These are for later in case you get peckish.'

He whispered something to my mother, something I failed to hear. She replied to his

words: 'There but for the grace of God.'

He turned round at the foot of the stairs and waved one of his crutches up at my mother. She was dabbing her eyes with the edge of her apron.

The door closed.

I wanted to talk to John on the way to Main Street, but I couldn't think of anything to say to him. Finally, sensing my unease, he asked: 'And what is your favourite subject at school then, son?'

'History,' I told him. 'I like the Greeks and the Romans and all the stories.'

He smiled at this. 'Oh yes, there are plenty of stories there to keep you busy.'

He spoke about his own childhood and upbringing, about his brothers and sisters, and before we knew it we stood at Main Street and at the entrance to the park.

'I'll say goodbye now,' he said. 'Tell your mother her thoughtfulness will remain in my heart forever.'

I swallowed and nodded, noticing something unfathomable in his eyes. He reached into his inside coat pocket and brought out a dirty little bag, tied with a shoelace. He handed it to me before turning for the park.

'Something for you, son. Don't ever lose it.'

I took the mangy little bag from him and promised I would look after it, whatever it was. I then headed for the corner grocer's, watching him from time to time as he hobbled through the park on his way to God knows where. I felt some regret. There were loads more things I would have liked to ask him; I sensed he was someone with many stories to tell.

'What's this?' my mother enquired when I put the bag on the kitchen table.

'He said I shouldn't lose it. I haven't opened it, so I don't know what it is.'

My mother picked the bag up and held it in her hand. She untied the shoelace and emptied the contents on the table.

Her face turned white and she stood motionless, staring at the revealed object.

'My God,' she whispered. 'It's the Victoria Cross.'

'Victoria Cross?'

'Son, we've just had lunch with a hero.'

Peter Mackay (b.1953)

Learning to Read

I guess it all started with my innate love of puzzles. We lived in an upstairs flat and, as a four-year-old child, I had to be 'kept quiet' to avoid annoying the neighbours on the floor below. So my dad used to bring me home jigsaw puzzles, which were cheap and cheerful at the time. I became quite proficient at these, even really large ones. To this day, I can remember my favourite as being *The Festival of Britain 1951*, of 500 pieces which I did over and over again. My mum and dad thought I was some kind of budding genius, but that wasn't really true, as I was quite daft in other ways – I just loved puzzles.

Then I started school and was quickly introduced to those wonderful puzzles called 'words'. I must admit that I learned to read proficiently by the age of six and I was the first one in my class to get to grips with it. You see, to me 'words' were just another terrific puzzle – and I loved them from the start.

I can almost exactly remember the precise moment when it happened.

My dear teacher, Sister Teresa had written a long word on the blackboard. She asked the class to spell it out. It was p-o-l-i-c-e-m-a-n. No-one volunteered; the length of the word alone was scaring them off from all they had learned. We were currently studying *Ann and Jim* books and this was the longest and scariest word we had ever seen without accompanying pictures.

I studied the word long and hard and got as far as 'polik' by mentally spelling it out. Then I suddenly remembered that 'CE' together is pronounced as 'S' – then the rest was easy. I shot my hand up, 'Please Sister, please Sister – please...' I was jumping up and down in my seat with excitement, and almost fell off the chair.

'Yes, Bernadette,' she said, kindly. No-one else had put their hands up at all, but I guess she didn't expect them to.

'It's POLICEMAN,' I said, to her stunned admiration.

After that, there was no stopping me. I read everything in sight. It was like a whole new world had been opened to me. I read sauce bottles on the table and cans of beans in the cupboard. I read traffic signs and shop headlights and even my dad's newspaper from the back when he was reading it (he told me off about this and said it was very bad manners). My parents took to hiding the Sunday papers so that I couldn't read them. I then joined the local library and read myself silly. You see, even after words had ceased to be puzzles, they still intrigued me beyond measure.

To this day, the written word still holds its fascination, whether it be composing a verse or story, or compiling a crossword. That's why writing never seems like hard work to me. It's my *raison d'etre*.

Vive les mots.

Bernie Morris (b.1946)

Lost and Found

I started school at the tender age of four. As there were no junior schools close to where I lived it meant that a short bus ride would have to be used. On the first day my sisters and brother took me with them to their school initially, and then put me on a bus to my new school, informing me very carefully that Dad would be waiting at the bus stop for me when I came home.

I really enjoyed going to school this first day as it was an exciting change to get out of the house and make so many new friends. Having a hot, freshly cooked meal at lunch time whilst eating with the rest of the children came as an added treat.

The day seemed to fly by and home time came around all too soon. I half-heartedly found myself with all the other children being shepherded onto the school bus to take us home. The ageing diesel powered bus groaned and rattled along at a very sedate pace dropping children off at various stops along the way.

All seemed to be going okay until I discovered, to my horror, that I was the last one left on the bus. I tentatively approached the stern looking lady, who seemed to be in charge, to say that I was lost! She then informed me that I would have to get off the bus! Although she kept asking me where I lived, I was really confused and scared by this time and for the life of me no matter how hard I tried, I just could not remember. So I got off the bus anyway in what seemed like the middle of nowhere. The bus shuddered and spluttered off, leaving me surrounded by a cloud of choking diesel smoke. I promptly plonked myself down on the kerb edging of the busy roadway, feeling really scared now, visibly shaking and crying my eyes out. Thankfully, after a short time had elapsed, a guardian angel duly appeared in the form of a nice lady who enquired what on earth the problem was and where I lived. Between sobbing my heart out through floods of tears, I tried to tell her but she did not understand; she then took me to a nearby house where the local policeman and his wife lived. They gave me a drink of milk and a biscuit to calm me down while they considered the problem, at the same time finishing off their evening meal. After what seemed like a lifetime in this strange house, but in reality was only a couple of hours later, there came a loud rat-a-tat knocking on the front door. Oh what joyous relief! It was my sister and mum. They had knocked on practically every door on the estate before a lady informed them that she had seen me and, that I was taken to the policeman's house by another lady who lived nearby.

I was so overwhelmed with joy and happiness to see my mum and sister after my great teary eyed adventure that I held Mum's hand as tightly as I could all the way home.

My Dad got the full broadside, ear bashing treatment from my mum, who gave him a good telling off and kept him in the doghouse for a long time after that little episode. After seeing that I was not there, my dad should have at least enquired after me when the school bus arrived at my destination outside of my siblings' school gates, but amazingly, he had not!

The next day I was adamant that I did not want to go to school any more. Mum forcibly escorted me on to the local bus and informed my school teacher what had happened the previous day. I melted into a screaming and crying session and dug my heels in as Mum dragged me into the classroom; she eventually left me after explaining to me quietly and calmly that everything would be okay.

Having none of it, I tried to run and escape, screaming, throwing myself at the now locked door for all I was worth, kicking and crying. I refused to take my coat off until I had calmed down a good deal later. The teacher reassured me that I would not be left on my own again in future and that I would go home on a different bus. The lady who had turfed me off the bus was severely disciplined about telling a new pupil of only four years old to get off a bus, unescorted, in a strange location. From that day on if I happened to be unfortunate enough to be travelling on her bus, she completely distanced herself from me with dirty looks to kill whenever we managed to make eye contact.

Luckily I soon regained my confidence when travelling to school by bus, but occasionally getting home had different challenges. Arriving close to my home destination outside the school where my sisters and brother attended, I had often been able to take a shortcut through the playground and find my way home from there. On this particular day, school had finished unusually early and the gates had been padlocked shut. I did not know the way around the school or an alternative route to the road I knew to take me home. A 'Knight in Shining Armour' or should that be a Fair Damsel? – A girl much older than me appeared in my time of need once again. She gave me a shin up and over the school gates back on my familiar shortcut route home. This diversion happened on various occasions, but time passed and I eventually reached the age of attending the same school as my sisters and brother.

It still gives me a cold shudder even now to think of that day so long ago as a tiny four-year-old, when I found myself stranded out in the big wide world in that scary, unfamiliar area.

Elizabeth M Clarke born 1951

My Grand-dad and the Trouble We Caused When Together!

Dad was never the same person when he returned home after the war, as I found out much later in life when it was all explained to me. That was probably the reason why I was sent to my Grandparents' house in the next street, for the weekends, holidays and Christmas each year. Mum knew I would have a good time with them and her three brothers.

The year of 1943 was quite a notable one. That was the year I appeared on the scene in south London, not far from Clapham Common. The timing could have been better, as London was in the midst of bombing, destruction and deprivation, but this was, with hindsight, a defining point in my existence. Anyone brought into the world at that time grew up to make use of whatever was available to them and not waste anything. We came through the remaining two years of war with as few scars as possible, and I have my Grandparents to thank for that. They doted on their first Grandchild despite his taking more than his fair share of the rations.

Chocolate was in very short supply, usually available from 'someone who knew someone' and I had the good fortune to be given a small square of this brown, sweet, melty stuff whilst still a baby in the pram. Nan had saved it as a special treat. As was the custom in those days, I was in my pram outside the front door on the pavement 'getting some fresh air' – it was considered safe, especially with Chip, the family dog, keeping guard between the wheels. I was part of his family and nobody would dare come within reach of the pram without chancing his set of teeth making painful contact. As with all toddlers given sweets, and not really knowing where my mouth was situated, my face became plastered with the chocolate, and Nan went indoors to get a face flannel to clean me up. Imagine her surprise when she returned to find my face spotless – Chip had jumped up and licked me clean to save her the job!

Since that day, I've always had dogs wanting to taste me!

Toys were also in short supply soon after the war and we had to make do and mend. From small marble-runs being painted and dried in the newly cleaned range in the kitchen (thus tainting any food that was cooked afterwards with the taste of fresh lead paint) to larger toys, such as scooters and go-carts (called Jiggers), the materials were usually found on the local bomb-sites where we foraged for anything 'interesting'.

Our finds included old pram wheels, planks of wood, washing line, shrapnel, bomb casings, and bottle tops – all useful stuff to make my first go-cart with the help of Grand-dad.

We wanted the 'bestest, fastest cart in the street' and to test it we, that is me, would ride down the road around the corner, which had a one in three gradient hill, from the top to the bottom, without falling off or anything breaking apart.

Come the day of the maiden voyage, Grand-dad and I went to the top of the hill with our pride and joy, to set off with a push from Grand-dad. No cars to worry about, as the only vehicle in the street was a hearse, brought home each night by a neighbour who was an undertaker... and he was working that day!

Yep. The cart was going fine, fast and furious for the 200-odd yards, but I had forgotten about the Coalman's horse and cart that stopped in his usual place at the T-junction at the bottom. There was nowhere to go but between the front and back legs of the horse, shooting out the other side with more than horse-belly hair on my head.

I had also forgotten something else. The horse usually emptied his bladder at that precise spot, filling the gutters with steaming yellow fluid, and I was duly soaked to the skin! Apparently the horse saw me coming, watched as I disappeared under him, turning his head to see me emerge the other side to witness my hitting the pavement and tipping out, the wheels making waves as it went through the puddle.

It wasn't bath night, as that was on Fridays with the tin bath in the back room, after everybody else had had their dip, making the water grey with suds and *Lifebuoy* soap. Between my crying and screaming (I hated baths) and the laughter from the grown-ups, I was eventually scrubbed clean and put into my uncle's bigger clothes whilst mine were washed, 'mangled' and put in front of the range to dry.

Funny really! It was the first time I'd had the chance to wear long trousers. Boys had to wear shorts all through the year until they were at least thirteen years old, according to school rules. Besides, there were no trousers available in the shops for little boys. My knees still bear the scars of past misadventures.

Grand-dad got it hot and holy for getting me into that mess – but he made up for it with plotting our next adventure. His new experiment was to make a big kite from bamboos found on a bomb-site, with some of Nan's material, obtained without prior consent or knowledge!

All went well on the Common until I was allowed to hold the string. The kite was too strong and powerful and it promptly lifted me off the ground, much to my delight! I hadn't gone more than a few yards when Grand-dad rugby-tackled me and brought us both crashing to the ground.

To steady his nerves he treated himself to a 'cup of tea and a fag' at the café/shed in the middle of the Common. I had to make do with an ice-cream! Ten minutes later we had our heads together planning the next bit of excitement.

Next on the production line was a scooter with steel ball-races (bearings) for wheels. They made a wonderful clattering sound as I sped down the hills over the flag stones, causing the neighbours to complain to Nan that 'Our Bert is on nights and he can't sleep with that racket'. I knew I was in trouble, but I didn't quite understand the concept of 'Night-work'. I thought everybody went to bed at night!

The scooter startled the Coalman's horse, so I never used it when he was around, and the milkman's horse almost bolted when I appeared mounted on the deafening contraption. Of those two horses, I adored the giant, dark Shire that pulled the red and blue coal-cart on its four brightly painted wheels. He would stand quietly as the coal was unloaded in black shiny sacks into the various houses to be stored under the stairs, the Coalman wearing his thick, leather, back protector and cap, keeping him from getting injured from the hundredweight sacks of broken sharp-edged fuel.

I was intrigued by this giant of a horse. He had his elevenses outside our house, and I would wrap my arms around his front left leg to give him a hug, despite being enveloped in the sweet-smelling moist atmosphere of digested hay puddling around our feet, his dinner-plate sized hooves dwarfing my little shoes. His great head with the splash of white down the front would slowly turn round to gaze at me with his big liquid brown eyes inside the blinkers, understanding that I was only knee-high to a grasshopper, and knowing to be careful not to hurt me. Sometimes he would give a contented snort, showering me with oat dust from the bag.

When his nose-bag was removed, ready to move on, he would let me wipe the oats from his face and nose, receive a pat and, with a mighty muscular flex of his great body, get the heavy cart moving to the next stop. The Coalman sometimes allowed me to walk with the horse along the road, and I hope the animal liked the company of a little boy. I can't remember his name, but the image of his gentle self is forever in my memory.

As for the Milkman's horse, he was a smaller, flighty, light brown animal. Never to put up with the likes of little boys hanging around, he would swing his head trying to knock me away. His eyes had a totally different look about them. The feeling was mutual. Although the milkman had complete trust in his capabilities, the creature just didn't like anything around him, be it boy, dog or cat.

Another delight was to follow the street-lamp lighter man with his long pole, adorned with a flame and hook right at the top. I was fascinated by the way he would appear through the gloom of the street to stop at each lamp post, reach up with his pole to open the glass door, turn on the tap with the hook, and light the hissing gas.

By the time he finished his round, the street was bathed in soft yellow light making all the colours soften and change, especially if there was fog in the air. The darkness between the lamps would hide the devastation of damaged homes and piles of rubble, making the area seem safer and cosier to my young mind. He always whistled the same tune, suffered my constant presence and questions and bade me 'Goodnight, God Bless' as he left for the next street.

Grand-dad had a workshop at home, filled with tools of all kinds, since he did jobs in his spare time for friends and neighbours who had suffered damage to their properties during the war. He worked for Westminster Council, doing any repairs to buildings and vehicles, so he had many skills under his belt.

It was heaven sitting on top of a pile of old newspapers (I would collect them from the street and get sixpence, that is 2.5p nowadays, in exchange at a local shop), watching Grand-dad fashion tools, toys, wood and metal items from any materials found, begged or borrowed. Every Sunday morning was taken up with cleaning and sharpening, tidying the workbench and showing me how to use the tools. He could always solve a problem, make anything that was wanted from the meagre supply of materials available, invent contraptions, build things for his beloved garden, including the constant repairing of the family's shoes and boots.

In his garden was a big solid structure that was the bomb-shelter. The walls were about fifteen inches thick, made from dark grey bricks with a solid concrete flat roof. A brown, wooden braced door allowed access to the dark interior which was kept immaculately clean, the only light coming from a three foot, ground-level grill that let fresh air waft through, keeping the air fresh and cool. There was a smell of creosote, wood, garden compost, and other unidentifiable smells that fired my imagination, and it became a 'secret den' that only I knew about!

Because it was a lot colder inside the shelter, even in summer, Nan kept her milk, butter (when she could get it from the shops) and meat in storage to prolong its life. Other stuff was stored in the corners and, on one memorable day, I found a big wooden train that Grand-dad had made many years ago for his own children. It was big enough to sit in the cab (if you were a small child), had loads of different sized wheels, a big metal funnel, and was painted green and blue.

My wheedling and begging eventually got the train into the daylight, and it must have measured some six feet long or more, and very heavy. One of my uncles decided he wanted some realism in our play; he put a smoking rag in the funnel and started pushing me up and down the concrete path in the garden. The speed at which we were going gave more air to the funnel, igniting the paraffin rag, leading to scorched paint, smoke and flames everywhere, and nearly giving Nan a heart attack! I found it exciting and added realism to the game!

Sadly, the train was put away after being doused with gallons of water, and could only come out 'when you two boys learn to behave yourselves'. That didn't stop me from creeping into the shelter when nobody was looking (or were they?) and playing with it, pretending I was in a never-ending tunnel going to Brighton, or somewhere else exotic!

And then there were my three uncles who lived at my Grandparents'. Their ages ranged from late teens to early twenties and they were just as bad as Grand-dad! Or should that read – as much fun as Grand-dad! Nan despaired of having 'five little boys who wouldn't grow up', but she forgave us for any problems we gave her – usually!

Although she was only four feet ten inches tall and very slim, she kept order in the household, deferring decisions to my Grand-dad, having made up her own mind first, and acted upon them before the 'men in the family made things difficult'. She was much loved, and she returned that love many times over. We never took advantage of her good nature... well, only sometimes... to get an extra biscuit or slice of bread and butter after school!

Although not having much money, no electricity in that part of London (gas mantles in every room) and only a range to cook on and keep the house warm, three bedrooms to share, no television (but we did have a relay radio), we five would find ways to make our lives exciting, find something amusing, and listen to each others' stories, either made up, or from books read to me at bedtime. Grand-dad never needed a book, as his stories were generally from memory.

There was always a big hand to hold when going about our business, big arms to have a hug from, and a soft muscular shoulder to snuggle against when feeling sleepy.

Rose tinted spectacles? No way! Life for grown-ups was hard, quality of life for children was dependant on the effects the war had on the grown-ups. In my case, I was lucky to have a loving mother and grandparents.

It's a pity that Dad wasn't involved much, but he did have his problems from the experiences of fighting on the Continent, with the resulting flashbacks that must have changed his character. I suppose he loved me in some kind of way, but he never showed much affection to my recollection. It was probably difficult to come to terms with going away for some years to return to his family which had an extra 'body' to look after, feed, clothe, and compete for Mum's affections. Reading social histories as an adult, I came to understand that this was a common problem which was not recognised and treated by the authorities.

Dad would have made a smashing sixth member of the gang, but the situation never became reality, which is something that I've regretted for many years.

There was, of course, the constant presence of good old Chip who guarded the family, the home, and the littl'un, offering a warm furry body to stroke and cuddle. He wasn't very big, came of mixed background, the terror of the street as far as other dogs and some of the awkward neighbours were concerned, but remained totally loyal to his adopted family. He was always the first into the bomb shelter, long before the air-raid sirens wailed their forlorn scream across the city, giving the grown-ups ample warning to respond.

Everything was alright with the world when we both settled together in front of the fire, to have a quiet nap, probably much to the relief of all the adults. It was very tiring keeping the big members of the family busy, and we had to recharge our energies on a regular basis!

Somehow dog and boy fitted together in a ball of peaceful innocence.

If asleep, neither dog nor boy was getting into mischief!

Until we woke up!

David Garrad (b.1943)

Nice Girls Don't

My mum said, at the age of fourteen I would be allowed out evenings, so long as I was home at a reasonable hour. I would also be allowed to go out with boys, providing they were nice boys, not like "those yobs down the alley." I knew she was referring to Bobby and the gang. As far as she was concerned, they were riff-raff or scum, or in my dad's opinion, "not worth a light." Bobby, in particular, worried my mum. She could see he had eyes on me; he made no effort to hide it. Whenever I happened to pass him by with my mum in tow, always the sweeping appraisal and the lecherous wink. She would say, loudly enough for him to hear, 'Don't ever have anything to do with that creature. You're too good for the likes of him.'

I would always look back at him and smile, if I was able to without Mum seeing, to show that I didn't share her opinion, though he knew that perfectly well, as I shortly discovered.

On one such occasion, my mum saw me looking back at Bobby. She didn't say anything right then, but when we got down the road a bit, she suddenly turned and slapped my head.

'Ouch!' I exclaimed, more surprised than hurt. 'Whassat for!'

She looked absolutely furious. 'Nice girls DON'T look at boys that way!'

'What way?' I stupidly asked.

'You know very what way well!' She was so mad, she was getting her words mixed up. That was a bad sign; she was really fuming. 'I saw how you were looking at that bloke, and you'd better not let me catch you doing it again!'

'I – I...' My argument trailed off. I wanted to say that Bobby wasn't a bloke – not just any bloke. He was my friend and he was a nice boy. But this would only have further incriminated me.

'I don't want to hear any more cheek!' she stated, emphatically.

That shut me up like a clam. Any form of verbal self-defence was regarded as 'cheek' and would be reported to my dad. Cheek to parents was a cardinal sin in those days.

But my mum's words had greater effect than she knew. 'Nice girls don't look at boys that way.'

'What way?' I wondered.

Nice girls don't look at boys...

Nice girls don't...

I worried about it all the way home. So I wasn't a nice girl. Could be I was going to grow up bad. But I didn't feel bad – it couldn't be wrong just to look at Bobby. All the other girls did. And I was his special friend – he said so. How could any girl help looking at him anyway? He was fine-looking.

Nice girls don't...

Later that evening, I looked at all the pin-up pics on my bedroom wall: Elvis, Cliff Richard, and Rick Nelson. They were all gorgeous. I think I liked Cliff Richard the best – he was sort of like Bobby. Was it bad to like pop stars? That was really just the same as looking at boys, wasn't it? Should I take them all down? Maybe I should ask my cousin Jon first. He was wise for his age; he would know the truth. But no – how could I ask him a thing like that? He might think I went around staring at boys all the time, and that wasn't true, was it? I couldn't picture any boy's face clearly except Jon's and Bobby's. Did that make me a bad girl?

My best friend, Mary wouldn't be much help either. She was just as dumb as I was about those sort of things. She didn't even know the obvious stuff like, you don't belittle a boy in front of his mates – you mustn't show him up that way. Male pride is fierce. I had to tell her these things, which came natural to me. So what could I do? I finally decided to ask Bobby himself. He wouldn't mind. He might tease me a bit, but he would tell me. He was older than Jon or Mary, and far more worldly-wise. Bobby would surely know if nice girls don't.

You'll never guess what he said...

Saturday, I got up early, and went to get my dad's morning paper before he woke up. This would be a good time to see Bobby. I knew he wasn't one to lie in bed when there was life to get on with. The weather was damp, but fairly warm. I pulled on a sweater over my jeans, then loped down the alley.

The ground was wet with recent rain. Congealed mud had settled in all the cracks and dips of the alley flagstones. This reminded me of school-dinner gravy – sort of lumpy with bits in, and I jumped over every squidgy looking place. I saw Bobby lounging in his own doorway with his best mate, Adam, and my heart sank a little; I'd hoped to find him alone – my question was important.

'Hey, look at that!' Bobby said as I skipped towards them. 'Don't she bounce nice?'

I stopped in mid-gallop, immediately conscious of my thin sweater, and no bra.

Bobby's grin almost reached his ears. 'I hope you're looking for me, darlin', 'cos I think you just found me.'

Adam's expression was fiendish. I wished he would go away. Not that I disliked him – I knew he was a good bloke. He was Bobby's best friend, so how could he be anything else? But his fierce eyes always unnerved me a bit. They seemed to bore right through me.

I managed to stammer through my blushes, 'I – I *am* looking for you, Bobby. I – I wanna ask you something important.'

He grinned so wide you'd have thought his jaw would fall off. 'Ask away, kiddo. This man knows everything.'

'I...' My voice sounded thin and peevish to me. 'I wanted to talk to you alone, Bobby.'

'Ain't it my lucky day, darlin'?' To Adam he said, 'Fade out, Shadow.' (Shadowcat was Adam's nickname.)

Adam said, 'You should ask me, little girl – not him. The Shadow knows it all.' His grin was still fiendish, but the intensity of his dark-eyed gaze was making me more nervous than ever. I shook my head, dumbly.

'I know what's on your mind,' he insisted. 'The Shadow knows.'

'Get lost!' Bobby told him. 'You trying to steal my bird?'

'Who me?' Adam's dark eyes widened and assumed the innocence of a bush-baby. But he began to move away, silent as a cat on his crepe-soled boots.

'Seeya, sweet!' he told me with a lecherous wink. Then he moved fast to avoid Bobby's well-aimed kick at his backside. They said there was no man faster than the Shadowcat, and I learned the truth of this much later.

But I knew they didn't mean it. Bobby and Adam were very close friends – closer than a lot of brothers I knew. They were worse than Mary and me.

'I'll git you later,' Bobby promised Adam's fast-moving shape.

'Bobby,' I said, 'I ain't your bird. You know I don't like that word. I ain't no feathered creature. I'm just a girl, Bobby, and I'm your friend. I need your wise head.'

I knew this pleased him by the way his eyes sparkled over his grin. 'What's up then, darlin'?' He sat on the doorstep and patted the space beside him to indicate that I should join him. 'Come and tell Bobby your trouble.'

I sat down beside him, gladly. I was lucky to have Bobby. He fulfilled the role of father, big brother, friend and confidant better than anyone else ever could. He was like my guardian angel.

'Bobby,' I began at once, 'the other day, when you saw me with my mum, she slapped me and she said, "Nice girls don't look at boys that way." What did she mean, Bobby? What way was I looking at you?'

He didn't reply at once; he seemed to be too busy grinning. Indeed, his grin was threatening to split his face. 'Oh, Jesus!' he exclaimed. 'Now I've really heard it all.' He continued his silent grinning, and then I noticed, with dismay, that he was actually shaking with suppressed laughter. It was the kind of helpless mirth that takes your breath away. He just couldn't speak with the force of it. My Bobby, my old mate – he was laughing at me!

My face flushed with colourful indignation, and I began to get up to run away. 'I shoulda known better,' I told him, hotly, 'than to ask a clown like you anything serious!'

He laid a restraining hand on my arm as his laughter finally escaped. 'Please don't go. Hee hee - har har! I'm gonna tell you. Hoo hoo - hee! I'm gonna answer your question - hee hee har! – in a minute – hee hee – I promise.'

I remained sitting beside him. Curiosity overcame my indignation. 'Bobby,' I pleaded, 'this kid needs your help.'

He then made a determined effort to be serious, even though the tears rolled down his cheeks and the corners of his mouth still twitched, still trying to laugh. 'Kitty-cat (that was his pet name for me), you're really killing me,' he said.

'Why Bobby? What's so funny? Please tell me.'

'I'm sorry I laughed,' he said, still grinning, 'I never meant to upset you, Kitty. You know I think the world of you - and I really wanna help.'

'Okay, Bob. I forgive you. Please go on.'

'You look at me with them big-baby eyes and you ask me that. That's what I found so funny darlin'. You was looking at me just the same way that you asked about.'

'What way, Bobby?' I gripped his shoulder. 'Please tell me. It's important to me.'

'Katie, I'm nuts about you. And I know that don't mean nothing to you right now - you're very young and confused.'

'I ain't confused. Get on with it, Bobby. Please!'

He smiled at my impatience. 'When you look at me with them big, beautiful eyes, they say to me, "Hey man, I think you're fine. Come a little closer."'

'What?' I was appalled. 'My eyes say that!'

'Yeah, kid, they really do. And don't think that I don't like the way you look at me - I love it. But I understand that you're just too young to control it. I realise it's just a primitive thing; like your little mate, Mary would say – it's a cave-man look.'

'Bobby, you're amazing me,' I said, wonderingly. 'I never knew girls did things like that, 'specially without even knowing. Does that mean I'm a bad girl, Bob? Like my mum said?'

'She never meant to say that you're a bad girl. She never explained enough. Square people often do that – they leave you wondering. She was trying to warn you that boys might think you are bad if you look at them that way. You see, Katie, there's a lotta blokes in this world who don't think about nothing 'cept the deep raging fire in their pants. A boy like that would take that look as encouragement. You gotta be careful, my darlin'.'

Well - wasn't he just wonderful? My great big, teasy-weasy, gorgeous, impossible Bobsky. I saw with terrifying clarity exactly where I'd gone wrong. Bobby explained things so well; I'd been right to come to him. I hugged him, impulsively. 'Thanks, Bobby. I'm glad you don't think I'm bad.'

He hugged me back, fiercely. 'You ain't no bad girl. You're the loveliest girl I know, and you can give me big-baby eyes any time.'

Adam re-appeared with his usual suddenness, as if he'd just teleported, and with my dad's newspaper. How had he known I intended getting one? 'Put that little girl down!' he scolded. 'She's jail bait!' (He was all of sixteen years old himself.)

Bobby released me, and jumped up to beat Adam's grinning head. The smaller boy barely had time to hand me the newspaper before it rolled with him, into the mud. I left the two of them, scuffling playfully, and getting their clothes filthy in the process. Boys! Why did they always act like little kids, no matter how old they got?

So, my mum had been right when she'd said, "Nice girls don't". They certainly don't go around making eyes at every boy. But then, she hadn't known that Bobby wasn't just any-old boy – he was my friend.

"Big-baby eyes" he called it. I smiled at the thought. A big baby? Was that how he thought of me? Couldn't really blame him for that; he was much older than I was. I didn't mind Bobby thinking me a baby. He looked after me very well and was always willing to help.

But I was still peeved that my mum thought wrong things about him. This was most unjust. She didn't know Bobby like I did; she'd never even spoken to him. She knew only that he wore a battered old leather jacket, which instantly labelled him the arch-villain of London. And his hair was too long. She couldn't see the heart of gold that beat beneath this rough exterior. It taught me well, never to judge a book by the cover.

Bernie Morris (b.1946)

Nightmares

Firestarter: My earliest recollection of a recurring nightmare was one which seemed able to invade any normal dream just by my thinking about it. It got to the stage that whenever I found myself dreaming, I would desperately try to avoid thinking about fire, because as soon as the dream became lucid and I realised that I was dreaming, it would start. Yes, in my dreams I started fires; I made them happen, even though I was terrified of the idea and didn't want to do it.

I'd be happily dreaming an ordinary everyday dream, usually situated in the top floor flat where I lived with my mum and dad; then suddenly I'd remember that I was a potential destructor. I would close my eyes tightly to avoid looking at any piece of furniture, but usually it was too late; whatever I'd last looked at would burst into flames. Then I would cry myself awake as the fire engulfed the room.

In the cold light of day, I could never understand what caused this abnormal fear. So far as I knew, I'd never had any reason to be afraid of fire, at least no more than anyone else has a healthy respect for it. I'd never had an accident, nor been burned or scalded or even played with matches. It was a complete mystery to me.

Years later, an astrologer told me that "fire" in our dreams indicates energy and potential and that mine just needed an outlet. Who knows?

The Witch who came Through the Ceiling: This was weird because I always thought I was awake at the time. I'd be lying in my makeshift two-foot wide bed, which was really just a converted settee, with the street lamp shining through the window, providing the only light apart from the dying embers of the coal fire which threw eerie shadows everywhere. I would be staring up at the ceiling which suddenly looked amazingly white in the surrounding darkness. Then a small black point would appear in the centre of the ceiling. This began to force its way downwards, with a grinding sound, becoming progressively wider, until it was recognisable as an upside-down witch's hat. At this stage I just wanted to hide my head under the bedclothes like most scared kids do, but I knew that if I did that, the witch might get through and capture or eat me, or whatever bad witches do. So I did the next best thing; I screamed and wailed until I woke up. I often wonder what would have happened if I had not been able to wake up in time.

My Mum didn't want Me: I guess this was my scariest nightmare of all and it happened about the age of six-seven years, after my little sister had been born.

I was lost, but then I saw Mum walking down the street towards me. She was wearing a gabardine mac and pushing a green pram which I knew contained my baby sister. I was so glad to see her, but she looked so terribly angry. I guessed I'd done something wrong again. But then she walked right past me, as if she didn't see me, or even know I was there. It really seemed like I did not exist. Like usual, I woke up crying.

Later in life, when I became quite adept at interpreting dreams, I realised that this was just my own insecurity and jealousy at the birth of my sister.

The Minotaur: As if these last were not bad enough, years later as a parent, I was most spooked by my eldest son's recurring nightmare. Richard was about eight-nine years old at the time. I would hear him crying, then rush upstairs to comfort him. But he didn't seem to be even aware of me; he would be pointing at something over my shoulder that only he could see. Sometimes he would tell me what he saw. He told me there was a bull with flaming eyes, sitting on a throne and glaring at him. There were also thousands of other bulls, sitting around, like in an arena, all staring at him. At this time, Richard was much too young to have ever heard the myth of the Minotaur in Crete, so I could not imagine where he had got the idea from. But I know it scared me witless.

Bernie Morris (b.1946)

No Fish and Chips

I still have a weird built-in program of meal-related memories which are only fading in pieces... that is, I can't remember the full week's menu.

'Cos we were dirt-poor, we always ate the same meals on the same days so Mum could budget for the week. I used to have to go to the shop for the stuff down the lane on Saturdays. 'Three lean loin pork chops please,' was my mantra in the butchers. These were for Sunday. Naturally Dad got the biggest even though he never ate his until the evening, having been out on the booze most of the day, and after it had been warmed in the oven with the gravy caked and hardening around the edges.

Thursdays I remember particularly as being "sausage, egg, chips and beans" night which we ate while watching *The Prisoner*, a program by which I was absolutely fascinated. I remember the many times I asked if I could have tinned tomatoes as well but Mum would say no because that was "part of another meal". Also I could never have the crust off the bread until it was nearly all gone because the crust "kept the bread fresh". Guess what one of the first meals was that I had after I left home and got married. AND I had the crust off a brand new loaf with it.

Odd how childhood memories intrude...

One time I remember vividly was when my mum could not take the beatings and the constant worry over money any more so she left home. That left me in the house mostly on my own (at about the age of thirteen) while Dad was out on the piss as usual.

One night I got in from school and I was ravenous. I searched the house for food and all I could find were a few spuds that were so old, they were sprouting, but I peeled and chipped them nevertheless. Our stove was gas-powered and the gas was on a meter which had, of course, run out. The electricity was paid quarterly, however, and had not yet been cut off for non-payment of the bills. It was time to try and be resourceful. We had one of those wedge-shaped single bar electric fires in the junk room, so I dug it out and wedged it between two house bricks from the yard so that the grille pointed upwards. I then bent the grille as close as I could to the element without it touching – my electrical knowledge was limited at the time but I knew enough to know that the grille MUST NOT touch the element.

I balanced the chip-pan (which had solidified lard in it rather than oil like people use nowadays) on the bent-in grille and plugged in the electric fire and waited. I let it heat up for a whole hour before I put in the chips, but as I put them in, I knew that the experiment was doomed as there was no "sizzle" followed by bubbling fat – more of a sigh. I left them to cook for another hour and then took them out. I tipped them on to some toilet paper on a plate as I could see that they were loaded with fat. I ate them because I was so hungry, but they were disgusting.

It was only in later life that I realised I might have had more success had I cleaned the parabolic reflector behind the element that was caked in grime and therefore absorbing the heat rather than reflecting it, but there y'go. I still eat chips, but not very often.

Jim Ollerhead (b.1955)

No Thanks for All the Fish

It was my first week at The English Martyrs RC Primary School which was run by the Sisters of Mercy (without any). I had been forewarned by Mum that you had to be "very good" at school, or else you would "get the cane". Although I was not quite sure what this meant, it sounded pretty ominous, and thus far I knew I hadn't done anything naughty, or "committed any sin" as my teacher so strangely put it.

So it was Friday lunchtime, always referred to as "dinner time" in those days. All the children were seated at tables for six in the large dining hall, through which the smell of fried fish pervaded from the steamy kitchen hatches at one end. Several of my classmates wrinkled their noses in distaste, and I must admit that I was doing the same. I guess that was my first sin. David-who-sat-next-to-me-in-class said wisely, 'You've got-to eat fish on Friday 'cos it's wrong to eat meat. Don't you like fish?'

'I dunno,' I said. 'Mum always gives me egg on Friday.'

'SILENCE!' roared Sister Dominica, who had just stridden into the hall with her black robes billowing. 'There will be NO talking at the table!' She now stood on stage at one end of the hall, glowering down at her diminutive pupils, all suitably cowed and awestruck. 'Now STAND for Grace!' she commanded.

Of course we did, and stumbled through the words, as most of us had not yet learned them correctly. It went something like, 'For what we are about to receive, may the Lord make us thankly trueful. Amen.'

At least Sister Dominica seemed satisfied with this garbled attempt. 'Now be seated and enjoy God's bounty,' she said. 'And remember that waste is sinful; It is an insult to the Lord!' With that she turned and billowed out again. I guess her duty was done.

We sat down and the dinner ladies began to come round with trays of plates. There was no choice involved – you were expected to eat what you were given. I remember that we "infants" were not allowed knives, only a spoon and fork was set out for each place, and there was no water to drink, which might have helped.

I stared aghast at the plate in front of me. There was a large piece of greasy battered fish, which looked most alien to my eyes, two blobs of mashed potato with grey lumps in, and a scoop of hard, bullet-like peas. I was hungry, but this did not look at all appetising to me. Glancing up at my companions' faces, I could tell that they felt the same.

Miss Murray was on patrol. She was not a nun, but I guess a kind of "special needs" teacher who also took a turn as dinner lady. I remember that she always wore a fur coat, very thick glasses, and carried two wooden rulers (her secret weapon). In her way, she was just as formidable as Sister Dominica. 'Eat up!' she barked as she passed each table of reluctant young diners.

So I picked up my fork, determined to be good and not to "insult God". I managed the mash and peas fine, then began to negotiate the dreaded fish.

The first mouthful confirmed my worst fears. Apart from the too-greasy batter, the fish itself was hard, dry and sprouting bones. I spent the first five minutes fishing some of the bigger ones out of my mouth and laying these at the side of my plate. I continued in like manner and with great effort until every last morsel of my fish had gone. I still don't know how I never threw up – I guess it was all down to my inherent determination (or stubbornness, if you like). Finally, I laid down my fork and spoon with a sigh of triumph. I guess that was my first sincere feeling of human achievement in the face of adversity, and I gloried in it for a few moments – but not for long.

The other kids on my table, including David-who-sat-next-to-me-in-class, had noticed my demolition of the meal, so immediately assumed that I must have liked it. Almost as one, in spite of my protests, they piled their uneaten fish onto my plate, then all sat there, grins on their faces, waiting for their empty plates to be collected. I didn't know whether to laugh or cry at that moment, but unfortunately for me, Miss

Murray came to our table just then and looked at my filled plate as well as all the empty ones.

'YOU are a wicked, ungrateful girl!' she told me. 'You are the only one here who has refused to eat God's precious food!' Then she raised her two rulers and brought them down sharply across my knuckles. The pain of this brought tears to my eyes, but more painful still was the way that my classmates looked down at their plates and said nothing. They were all too scared to admit what they had done.

I felt betrayed at that time, but since then I have realised that you can't really expect five-year-olds to have developed a sense of loyalty; they were just scared kids after all. Miss Murray however, I do blame. I know she wore thick glasses, but how could she not have seen that a five-year-old kid does NOT get dished up five battered fish?

Funnily enough, I love fish now and all forms of seafood (except for battered fish).

I still hate injustice, however.

Bernie Morris (b.1946)

Off the Road

The Second Life of Lun

It was a fine September evening around 7.30 pm and still daylight.

My mum was working late shift, and I, aged thirteen, was supposedly home with my dad; but quite naturally, was out and about on such a pleasant evening. Having just received my pocket money, I decided to cycle to the local off-licence, this being the only shop open at that time. I knew that cycling on the road was forbidden in the evening, as there were no lights on my BMX bike; so although it was still daylight, I rode along the pavement – there were not too many shoppers about to complain. I cycled along happily, thinking of all the crisps, cokes and chocolate bars I was about to devour, which Mum wouldn't know about.

Imagine my shock and disbelief when a parked and driverless car suddenly began to hurtle towards me!

I had no time to take evasive action. My bike and I were thrown right through a nearby hedge and halfway up someone's front garden, demolishing several previously well-ordered flower beds along the way, and landing in a painful tangled heap almost on the doorstep.

During the daze which followed, I heard the owner of the garden threatening grievous bodily harm to a van driver who had hit the parked car for no apparent reason.

I was duly taken to hospital, and my mangled bike was retrieved by my older brother, George. My mum received one of those horrendous phone calls at work which every parent dreads: "Your son has had an accident..."

I received fifteen excruciating stitches to my damaged knee, which fortunately was my worst injury. Mum held my hand all the while, and I'm proud to say that I was very brave – she cried more than I did.

The police informed us later that the van driver had actually fallen asleep at the wheel, thereby failing to swerve to avoid the parked car. I was very lucky to be alive. If I had been walking instead of cycling, I wouldn't be here to tell the tale. My mum reckoned this was one of my nine lives again.

We often talk of this bizarre incident. I am still convinced that I must be the only boy in the world who was knocked down by a parked car whilst cycling on the pavement.

Do you think I should go for the *Guinness Book of Records*?

Lawrence Palmer (b.1975)

Peter Rabbit

When I was about eight or nine, my dad brought home a beautiful black buck rabbit which he said was for me. I had never been allowed to have a pet before, and was overjoyed. I loved the rabbit at once, and named him Peter.

Although we lived on the top floor of an ancient Victorian building, we were fortunate enough to have access to a flat roof. This proved a very good substitute for a back yard, and this was where Peter was kept, in his hutch.

My dad said I had to look after the rabbit all by myself, and I was very glad to do this. No pet was ever more cosseted than Peter. I would brush his fur until it gleamed like black velvet and put fresh hay in his hutch every day while I let him out for a gallop in his pen (this was an old playpen covered in chicken wire which my dad had made). I would have taken him out for a walk on a lead if I had been allowed. And Peter had only fresh green food – nothing dried. On market days, after school, I would collect from beneath the stalls parsnip and cauliflower tops (discarded in those days). And between times, I would forage in the bommies (bombed ruins of London) to find dandelions, groundsel or clover. It was then that I began to study books about wild plants to discover which ones were good for rabbits. Peter grew big and strong, but he was still gentle. He would eat right out of my hand, and always greet me with a soft woffley nose trying to poke through the wire of his hutch. I was a lonely child, and Peter became my best friend in the world.

Then one day after school, there was another hutch on the roof. This housed a black and white female rabbit. I promptly named her Bonnie; but my dad said I mustn't take her out of the hutch to play like I did with Peter; she wasn't as tame as he, and might try to run away and fall off the roof. This seemed like sensible advice and I obeyed. I fed Bonnie just as faithfully as I did Peter, but my dad did the necessary hutch cleaning and exercising – never at the same time as Peter, I noticed.

After that, Peter began to change. He seemed to become moody and irritable; he wouldn't let me cuddle him any more. And one day when I opened the hutch to lift him out, he kicked at me with his strong hind legs and raked my arms with his claws, producing several nasty long red scratches. I was naturally upset by this strange behaviour from my pet, and thought perhaps he was jealous of the other rabbit. 'But I still love you, Peter,' I told him. 'You are my friend.'

A few days later, Bonnie was allowed to play in the pen with Peter, and after that he became gentle again, though not quite as friendly as before. I was relieved. Peter must have been lonely – that was why he'd been so cross. But a strange thought occurred to me: Why did Peter need another rabbit when he had me? I didn't need other children, did I? I had no friends at that age. I was a bit of a loner at school, and was never allowed out to play in the evenings. My little sister was only three at the time, and although I was very fond of her, she wasn't much of a playmate as yet. There was only Peter. I began to feel a bit jealous myself.

Then came the terrible day when I came home from school to find Peter's hutch empty, and Bonnie playing alone in the pen. I hurtled down the attic stairs, and had to go to the bathroom because I suddenly felt sick with fear – Peter must have escaped and fallen off the roof. We lived four floors up – he would surely have been killed. My fears were realised in a worse way than I'd imagined. There in the bathroom, I froze with shock. Suspended by its hind legs from the ceiling, right over the bath, was a large black rabbit – quite dead. A small globule of congealed blood glistened from its nostril. Surely this could not be Peter? Not MY Peter. Not my beautiful warm cuddly little friend!

I think I began to scream and cry at that point, because my mum rushed in and told me not to be silly. That wasn't Peter. Dad had bought that rabbit at the butcher's for Sunday dinner. Peter had run away into the park and was now happy with lots of other rabbits. I shouldn't be such a baby.

I almost believed her because I wanted to; I couldn't bear to think that Peter was dead – yet I didn't quite believe her. I held my agony inside for two days.

Sunday dinner was duly served in the form of casserole, which we often had. It was chicken, my mum tried to tell me. But in my heart, I instinctively knew this tender white meat was Peter; and I could not have eaten a single bite without choking to death. I glared at my dad with the first open defiance I had ever shown. HE was the murderer. All of the times he had beaten me were nothing compared with this. At that moment, I hated him.

I was duly slapped and sent to bed for this sullen behaviour. But it didn't seem to matter. I just wished childish curses upon my dad and cried for Peter.

A few days later, my mum tried to explain to me. Peter had only been bought to make baby rabbits. Bonnie was soon going to have babies – we'd have lots of new rabbits – I could have another one.

I didn't understand how grown-ups could be so cruel. Why had they told me Peter was mine? Why had they given me that wonderful gift just to snatch it back again? Didn't they understand about love?

The baby rabbits were born, and at first I thought they were horrible – naked and squirming – like sausages with tiny feet. But in a few weeks they were furry and cute. There were two white ones, two black and white like Bonnie, and one – only one, black like Peter.

'Would you like that one?' my dad asked me.

'No!' I told him curtly. 'I don't want ANY. They are all yours.' And I swore to myself at that moment that I would never ever keep another pet.

For love brings only pain.

Bernie Morris

Piece/Peace of Mind

One morning while eating my breakfast cereal, I heard my mother say on the telephone that she was going to give someone "a piece of her mind". I had never heard that expression before, and was quite impressed with it. It sounded so grand and important.

A few minutes later I was on my way to school (first grade) and came to the school crossing. The crossing guard held up his hand for me to wait, but I ignored him and skipped gaily across the street. When I got to the other side, he grabbed my arm and said, 'I ought to report you to the principal.'

I sassily replied, 'Go ahead. I'll give her a piece of my mind.'

The next thing I remember was sitting on a hard bench outside the principal's office, feeling full of gloom and doom; I had never been in trouble at school before.

When I was finally sent in to see the principal, I faced a stern woman sitting behind a desk. I stood quivering before her. 'Well,' she said, 'I'm waiting.'

'What are you waiting for?' I managed to croak.

'For you to give me a piece of your mind,' she said.

I felt so mortified and embarrassed that I started to cry and said, 'I can't. I don't know how.'

She smiled and kindly said, 'What would you rather have – *peace* of mind or a *piece* of my mind?'

I shook my head, hardly knowing what she was talking about. But then she explained...

Barbara Tepper (b.1935)

The Pink Dress

It must have been around my tenth birthday that my mum bought me a lovely pink dress and, I was particularly proud to wear it for the first time, (I was always given hand me down clothes from my two older sisters), except for the time I remember another beautiful cotton dress that I had. I must have been aged around six years old at the time. I absolutely adored that dress too and wore it at every chance I got. It had little guitars in a random odd spot type of pattern all over it and, I always felt happy when I wore it.

I eagerly slipped into my new pink dress and immediately started strutting my stuff, singing to myself, walking and skipping along with great pride. My friend called round for me just when I was in full flow, super model posing mode. "What a lovely dress," she exclaimed as I beamed with even more pride on the front doorsteps. We then skipped down (me still beaming with pride) the long garden path together holding hands, me promptly tripping over the edge of a protruding flagstone. I went flying headlong to the ground with a sickening crump, and promptly gashed the underneath of my chin wide open on the pathway.

What is that old saying? "Pride cometh before a fall!" Beside myself with grief, as blood poured out all over my lovely new dress, my mum came rushing out of the house clutching a tea towel to stem the tide of blood. "What have you done you silly girl?" she exclaimed in a near panic.

I felt pretty sick with stars whizzing round my head at that stage and could only manage a tearful response, "I've bled all over my new frock!" I wailed. Being particularly unflustered about the amount of blood that was emanating from the deep wound and more concerned about my new dress, which was now totally ruined, of course. The second stage shock of the accident then kicked in as my limbs melted into jelly and I went all floppy. My mum then had to virtually half carry, half drag me to the hospital for five stitches to be sewn into my chin, a very painful procedure I didn't want to repeat any time soon I remember. I went to school on the Monday morning feeling very sorry for myself whilst at the same time sporting a rather large bandaged dressing that covered half my head!

Mum started working extra hours to cover the growing household bills; she did not have much free time now and even less time to stand in the cellar at the copper boiler we had always used to manually wash our mountainous piles of clothes. Mum did however manage to get a new washing machine (a Rolls Rapide). The machines were made in Cricklewood, London, and were marketed as an 'Automatic Twin Tub,' costing around £60 c1961-2. Mum couldn't afford to buy ours though as that amount was a king's ransom to us. A man came around every week in a green Morris 'Z type' van and, loaned out the machine for an hour at a time to mum and our neighbours. This was now a much quicker, easier and more efficient way to wash our weekly mounds of laundry.

Although I did stubbornly persist in a vain attempt to wash the blood stains out with the rented washing machine, my new dress defied all my dogged efforts at stain removal and was sadly but inevitably, consigned to the rag and bone man's cart.

Elizabeth M Clarke, born 1951

Polio Jab

I, Bobby, always looked up to my elder brother, Billy who was eighteen months older, but to me he seemed much older than that. Billy was always playing with the big boys – always playing brave games.

Billy never wanted me to play with him. He thought, just like everyone else, that I was a silly little scaredy-cat. Only I, Bobby knew that inside, I was really as brave as a lion cub. I just didn't show it – that's all.

But this day, Billy and I were playing together; we were on a scary adventure. This was only a trip to the doctor's on the bus, but to Billy and especially me, it was an adventure indeed.

'Why are we going to the doctor's, Mum?' I asked with some trepidation.

'Oh, it's only for a polio inoculation, that's all. Nothing to worry about,' she soothed.

'Inoculation?' I wondered, and looked quizzically at Billy.

'It's a jab,' he whispered back, knowingly.

'Jab?' I queried, nervously.

'Yeah, they stick this dirty great needle in yer arm,' said Billy with a horrible smirk on his face.

I knew he liked doing it – just scaring me, so it couldn't be as bad as all that.

'Now shut-up, the pair of you!' said Mum, rather crossly.

Billy and I remained quiet now, especially me – I'd already had my legs smacked that morning and didn't care for any more. That would only make me cry in front of big brother, Billy.

So, I began to daydream, keeping quiet, just letting my mind wander... I soon stopped though; this daydream was turning into a nightmare. In my mind, I could see this white monster with three eyes – the middle one blazing down at me. The monster had an inoculator in its hand, a strange object with a dirty great needle on it, which looked just like one of Mummy's meat skewers.

The lion cub had gone to sleep and I was dead scared. I wished I had Rupert with me. Rupert might have been just a tatty old teddy bear to everyone else, but to me he was a friend. I could cuddle him whenever I liked, 'cos Mummy didn't much like cuddles.

'Come on, you two!' she called, 'this is our stop.'

We got off the bus right opposite the doctor's surgery. As the bus trundled away, it disclosed a view of an imposing red brick building. A sign on the black door said "Doctor's Surgery", but I translated this as "Monster's Den".

The door creaked open...

I hung back and didn't want to go in, but Mum pulled me in, roughly. She didn't want any of my "nonsense". I looked up at her with what must have been a scared expression, while struggling not to cry. But there was no comfort in her eyes, just exasperation. To her, I was just the scaredy-cat boy. Why couldn't I be brave like Billy?

We sat in the waiting room: waiting. I looked around. There were lots of other children of our own ages, but what seemed odd was that some, in fact most of them, were sitting on their mum's laps or had her arm around them. They were scared, just like me, but they were being comforted. Why wasn't I? *What's wrong with me? I'm supposed to be brave, just like Billy.*

I looked at my brother. He looked a bit scared too, but I knew he wasn't really. Billy played brave games; he was already brave.

A nurse was calling out names and mums with their children got up and joined the queue that disappeared behind a curtain. Some of the children could be heard crying, others just moaned a bit, but none of them came out again. *Did the white monster get them?* Boy, was I scared!

Very soon the nurse called our names, 'William Smith and Robert Smith!'

'Go on then – it's your turn,' said Mum, without bothering to get up.

I looked at her, silently beseeching her to come with us; I didn't dare to actually ask. That would've made me look too babyish in Billy's eyes.

My big brave brother pushed me ahead in front of him. He wasn't going to go first if he could help it. Poor me; I was the guinea pig!

The queue was gradually diminishing; slowly and inexorably I was being drawn towards the dreaded white curtain which hid the monster with the inoculator. I turned and looked back at Mum once more, hoping for at least a reassuring smile, but she wasn't even looking our way. She just sat there, like a stone statue, quite unaware of the turmoil inside me.

I then glanced back at brother Billy whose name had just been called, but all I got was another shove forward and 'Go on, it's your turn!' He should have been at the top of the queue, but pushed me ahead of him through the curtain.

I just stood there, petrified, unable to move; I didn't dare to raise my eyes to look up at the monster, but I saw the inoculator in his hand. I gasped; the needle was as big as a skewer. I imagined it would go right through my arm and come out the other side.

The monster didn't say a word; and I couldn't speak either, because I sensed that Billy had crept in behind me to watch the proceedings, and I didn't want to show myself up to him, so I couldn't even scream. *Close your eyes, be brave, be brave!*

The monster grabbed my arm.

Be brave! Be a lion cub!

Jab! Ouch!

The monster let go. It was over.

I sighed with relief. *I did it! I did it! I was brave.*

I turned to share my elation with Billy, but he wasn't there any more. Then I heard the monster speaking my name – and he was grabbing my arm again.

I was terrified once more. *Everyone else has only one jab. Why must I have another?*

Yes, everyone should have only one polio jab; but our mother dressed us the same. The doctor was busy – too busy to know one brother from another. Now I really *did* need help. I frantically looked around for Billy, but he was nowhere to be seen.

Jab! Ouch! Too late, it was done.

This time it was much worse. The room swayed to and fro, round and round and got very dark. *I'm dying, the monster has killed me.* That was the last thing I remembered for a bit.

I opened my eyes, saw a kind face, heard a concerned voice. 'Hello young man, you had us worried for a moment, but you're all right now.' Her smile was warm and kind. But this was the nurse; she wasn't Mum. *Where is she?*

The nurse sat me up and gave me a boiled sweet.

I then saw my mum, still sitting in the waiting room, just like a stone statue, with Billy beside her, probably waiting for me to get over my scaredy-cat stupidity. I wondered if she knew about Billy's trickery. If she did not, then I certainly wasn't going to tell her. There was no way I would ever become a grass or a tell-tale. It was bad enough being a scaredy-cat.

It was about then that I realised there was something terribly wrong with my life – perhaps with me. Nobody actually loved me – nobody cared.

But *I* did. I loved and I cared about loads and lots of people and things. But I now knew that I mustn't ever show this kind of weakness. It had to stay locked inside me. My Dad was a military man, like most people's dads of my generation. He firmly believed in the British "stiff upper lip" and in bringing up his sons to be heroes and soldiers.

And as for my big, brave brother – I never quite looked at him in the same light again. He was the one who had chickened out of the polio jab and forced me to take the needle for him. Was that brave?

In later years, a wise teacher told me this: 'You are far braver than any soldier or hero, if you can do a good deed for someone else, even though you are terrified of doing it. To overcome fear is the bravest thing of all.'

I didn't know it then, but I had just started to build a barrier in my mind – that which would stifle my ability to love. As I grew older, I began to make sense of this coldness within me – and tried to fight it.
    But that's another story...

Anonymous (b.1950)

Remote Control

I was eleven or twelve years old and the eldest boy in a family of four. Like most elder brothers or sisters in those days, I had a certain amount of responsibility thrust upon me, which included some babysitting, running errands, household chores, and definitely making endless cups of coffee for my stepfather as soon as I was old enough to be competent. As he was out of work at this time, and my mum had an evening canvassing job, Dad's idea of helping around the house was to delegate chores to the kids – mostly me.

There was some compensation however; as the eldest I had the privilege of going fishing and to football matches with him. As a man of comparative leisure, he had the full advantage of being able to pursue his several hobbies long before retirement age. One of these was train-spotting in which I had not the slightest interest, but luckily for me, he always preferred to go this alone. But the football was great. It was cheap in those days as the local team had only reached the 4th division, so that dads could afford to take kids. I therefore got to go to most of the home games and occasionally some of the "away" ones too.

Fishing was also enjoyable once we'd arrived at the "swim". The only snag was that we didn't have a car back then, so I became the tackle porter. Sometimes it was quite embarrassing trying to board a bus, laden with bait boxes, keep-net, rod-cases, folding seats, etc, trying not to drop anything, especially on the way back when we would smell quite strongly of fishy river, but at least we usually got seats to ourselves.

Of all the times we went through the fishing season, my best memories are of "first night" usually around 16th June. Sometimes we'd take a few of my mates along if their parents allowed it. We would arrive about 9pm while it was still light enough to set up the gear, even more heavily laden than usual with flasks of coffee and piles of sandwiches to keep us going; then fish until dawn. On one such occasion, my friend Dean, aged thirteen, actually fell asleep on the river bank, toppled forwards and landed in the water with a terrific splash, which soon woke him up as well as the rest of us. Luckily, we had torches and lamps with us, or else we might not have found him in the dark. And as there was no transport home until 6am, we had to light a campfire on that occasion to prevent him catching pneumonia, and so that he could dry off a bit before his mum saw the state of him and blew her top.

So Dad was OK in some ways. The thing was he liked kids once they were old enough to be mates with, but thought the younger ones were just a pain in the arse, unless of course they were doing something useful – and that certainly wasn't by following his example. He actually stayed on the dole for about three years, from the time Mum got our first council house and my youngest brother was born, until the same kid was two and a half, then he finally decided to do a TOPS course in mechanical engineering and to marry my mum in order to pay less tax. Then even after he'd completed the course and landed a well-paid job, he was still very tight with money and refused to spend any on home décor, furniture or holidays.

Needless to say, we lived in a bit of a dump and grew up without any "mod cons" which most families were just beginning to take for granted. We just about had a second-hand fridge, but there was no washing machine, vacuum cleaner, or telephone. Those things did not materialise until my mum started full-time work when Lawrence (the baby) was five years old. Dad did buy a black & white portable television, after refusing to consider the cost of a colour TV licence, never mind the price of an actual colour set, which I must admit was pretty horrendous then. This small telly stood in pride of place on an old trolley table, opposite his favourite armchair, which was right next to the gas fire and a comfortable ten feet away from the screen. Dad was one of those laid-back types who didn't just sit in a chair, he collapsed and sprawled into it, and once he was ensconced there, he wouldn't move for the night. I can still picture him, staring at the flickering screen, idly flicking his fag ash in the general direction of the waste bin on his right, and usually missing it. And if he heard any of us kids come in through the back door, he'd immediately yell, 'Make the coffee!'

Which brings me to mention the funniest thing he ever did, to prove his extreme laziness, and which we still laugh about more than thirty years on.

It was a summer's evening and I was outside in the square playing footie with some mates. Mum was at work, the two youngest brothers had gone to bed and my sister was playing with her friends somewhere else. The only one indoors with Dad was Jim, then aged six or seven. The telly did not have a remote control; I'm not sure if they'd even been invented at the time. Young Jim was not allowed to touch the television as he had a knack of pushing wrong buttons and breaking everything. Dad must have quickly realised his predicament: that he would have to get out of his chair and walk ten feet across the room in order to change the channel. That's what we later surmised; he never actually admitted it.

Jim came to the front door in his 'jamas and yelled at me a few times, but I didn't hear due to all the racket we were making, besides which I am deaf in one ear. So Jim moved down the path to the gate, cupped his hands around his mouth and hollered, 'RICHARD – DAD SAID YOU GOTTA TURN THE TELLY OVER!'

Everyone stopped and stared at the little kid in disbelief; then we all fell about laughing.

My dad was definitely the laziest in the world. I guess I never quite lived that down.

Richard Quittenton (b.1965)

Rocking Horse

The telephone rings...

'Hello, Mr Moss?' a female voice enquires.

'Speaking,' I reply.

'Mr Robert Moss, son of Mr William Moss?' the voice asks again. This need for precise identification sets my alarm bells ringing.

'Yes, I am Robert Moss.' A slight tremor has crept into my reply.

'This is the ward sister of Chapel ward at Reading Hospital.' I begin to fear the worst. Her voice is soft and tinged with sadness. Desperately I cling to the phone, wishing I could slam it down. I don't want to listen, but I have to.

'I'm very sorry Mr Moss, but five minutes ago, your father died peacefully in his sleep.'

Dumbstruck, I listen to the details with barely a murmur. Finally, I find sufficient voice to say, 'Yes, I'll be there as soon as I can.'

Fifteen minutes later, I'm shown into the room where Dad spent his last days, and died alone. All the life support equipment has been removed, the lamp is dimmed, and a single red rose lies upon his chest. Dad looks very peaceful. There is a serene expression on his face. It's just as though he is asleep.

Suddenly it dawns upon me. Dad is asleep permanently! All those things I always meant to say and do – now it's too late, too damned late! Feebly, I whisper, 'Bye Dad,' with my eyes full of tears. I leave the hospital, knowing I will never see him again. That's it!

After the funeral, along with many other things, it fell upon me to sort out Dad's shed-cum-workshop. A place full of memories; they struck full force as soon as I opened the door. I gritted my teeth and waded into my task. I found rusted paint tins with rock hard contents, which went into the dustbin with many other items of no use. Other things, such as an old outboard motor that hadn't been used for years, went to a car boot sale. Then I found the tools: chisels, planes, saws and mallets. These had been much used by my dad, particularly for toy-making. Some of my best childhood memories were of the toys he had made, so I kept the tools.

After many hours of toil and reminiscing, I came across something large with an old blanket draped over it, tucked away in a dark corner of the shed. I grasped a corner of the blanket and whisked it off, which was a silly thing to do, for years of accumulated dust rose up to choke me. When my coughing fit had subsided, and the dust was finally settling, I rubbed my eyes and took a look. I couldn't believe it – my favourite toy – the best my dad had ever made: my rocking horse! All these years it had stood forgotten at the back of the shed, but now the memories came flooding back. "Champion" was his name. I caressed his now somewhat tangled mane. The leather saddle had grown a coating of mildew with the passage of time. I wiped this clean with a rag. 'One more ride just for old time's sake,' I whispered to myself.

I put one leg over Champ's back with greater ease than I had ever done as a child. I was much taller now, though luckily still light and wiry. I had aged in years since I had last sat in this old saddle, but was still a big kid at heart.

I just sat there for a bit, leafing through those distant memories of the times I had played on this wonderful horse. The adventures I'd had! One day dressed in my cowboy outfit, I'd galloped amongst imaginary Indians, six-guns blazing. Another time I'd been Richard the Lion-heart, cleaving the skulls of hordes of infidels with my sword Excalibur. Yes, I know that's King Arthur's sword, but those details don't matter when you're a kid.

But now I had been working for quite a few hours and was feeling rather weary, so I leaned forward to rest my head on Champ's scruffy mane. I'd never ever told my dad how much I'd loved this rocking horse, and I'd never even told him I loved him either. Now it was all too late.

A tear rolled down my cheek as I was filled with remorse once more.

My quiet sobbing gradually induced a gentle rocking motion, and weariness caught up with me. I must have drifted off...

My mum was sitting opposite me at the dinner table. 'Please may I leave the table?' I asked politely.

'No,' she replied. 'Wait until I've finished as well.'

I slumped in my chair and pretended to wait patiently, meanwhile pondering the unfairness of grown-ups being able to leave the table whenever they liked. Then there was a sharp rap on the window. Dad was outside, beckoning us both to join him.

'Come on Bobby,' Mum said, 'let's go and see what Dad wants.'

Brimming with curiosity, I followed Mum into the garden. As I stepped around the corner, I saw the rocking horse.

It was painted black and white in a piebald design, and on its back was a real leather saddle complete with a lasso hanging from the pommel. There was a bridle adorned with brass buckles and beautiful tasselled reins. Its eyes were bright, ears pricked forward, eager to be away, forelegs stretched out as if about to leap, and hind legs well back to push the miles away. I just stared in speechless wonder, until Dad said, 'How about a ride then Cowboy?' I nodded a reply.

Dad picked me up and hoisted me into the saddle. He gave Champ a shove, and I was away – having the time of my life. 'He's yours now, so look after him well.'

I wanted to hug my dad and say something special, but all I could think to say was, 'Thanks Dad.'

'Come and have your tea,' Mum said to Dad. 'Let's leave Bobby to play.'

I played all right. All that afternoon I barely left the saddle. Teatime came and went, and then it was bedtime.

The next morning, I awoke with a guilty feeling. I hadn't really thanked my dad properly. Champion was the best present I had ever been given. I loved him and I loved Dad for making him. But I was a rather reserved child. I just could not bring myself to actually say "I love you" to anyone, not even my parents. I knew if I tried to I would just get all embarrassed and clam up. I had to do something to show my appreciation, but what?

Inspiration came. I would write a note. That way I wouldn't feel embarrassed, and Dad would still know that I loved his present. So I wrote:

Dear Dad,

Thank you very much for making the rocking horse.

I think he's super, just great, like you.

I love him very much. I love you very much too.

love Bobby xxx

So now all I had to do was leave it somewhere for Dad. But where?

I had another good idea. Dad smoked and always took the cigarettes out of their packet and put them into his cigarette case. I would hide my note inside the case.

I crept into Mum and Dad's bedroom. The cigarette case was on the bedside table. I tiptoed across the room so as not to wake them (I was always awake first). Ever-so carefully, I opened the case and placed my note inside. I shut it with a barely audible click. Then disaster struck. I dropped the case onto the wooden floor – CRASH!

I sat up feeling dazed on the shed floor. I realised I must have dozed and then fallen off the rocking horse. But what a strange dream I'd had. It had seemed so real.

It was getting dark by this time, so I decided to call it a day in the shed. I went indoors, rubbing my head.

'Sit down Bob,' Mum said, 'I'll make you a nice cup of tea.' As she placed the tea in front of me, she said, 'While you were busy in the shed, I was sorting through some of Dad's stuff indoors. I thought you might like to have these.'

Amongst the bits and bobs in the plastic bag, I could see Dad's old lighter and cigarette case.

I waited until I got home before I dared to look inside the cigarette case. With trembling hands I opened it, and there inside was a note written in childish scribble – the same one I had dreamt about, but not quite the same. A footnote had been added: *I love you too, son.*

I think I probably inherited my natural reserve from my dad.

Robert Morris (b.1950)

Rowdy Haircut

Harry was a rare bird. He actually liked getting his hair cut on a Saturday morning even though the traditional barber shops were known to be very busy and overcrowded on that day.

This particular day there were fourteen people in the shop of which four were women, two hairdressers and two women with their children.

Everyone vaguely knew each other, 2 or 3 very well. Boredom is the biggest problem waiting to be dealt with hence Harry got reading an old edition of Readers Digest.

Harry burst out laughing, why asked many in the shop.

Let me tell you what I have just read, said Harry.

Marriage is that place between heaven and hell where men suffer for their sins.

Very funny but not to some of the women, one of the waiting mothers in particular started to moan about her husband's habits, dirty, out with the boys, doing nothing around the house and assumed Friday night was conjugal time.

That got two men answering back on the basis they knew wives as good time girls.

As soon as Dad came in from work, dog tired, they left him to get his own meal and look after the children, they were off for a good time night out with friends dancing and drinking.

The argument had begun and everyone seemed to jump in, everyone had an opinion.

The two women cutting hair joined in very forcibly, the poor chaps having their haircut jumped from the chairs; pleased they hadn't lost their ears!

Harry thought 'What have I done? I have come in for a quiet haircut and a bit of a gossip. Sitting near the door and worried what was going to happen, Harry thought I will hop out and bolted for the door!!

He missed that camaraderie and friendship with the staff for the next six months whilst he had his haircut elsewhere and then he would venture back – this time midweek, but he got a very frosty reception – they hadn't forgotten him, he was even less happy when Eve, the woman who usually did his hair virtually scalped him, he had little say in his normal trim – oh dear, perhaps the saying from the Reader Digest had an element of truth in it after all!

Brian Ward

RUTH – A Girl Like No Other

This true tale relates the adventures of a family member (names changed):

As a child Ruth lived with her father and his new partner. She learnt to be independent and self-sufficient. She is also outgoing, friendly, has caring nature and – is a vegetarian; luckily her personality hasn't changed over the years.

The Early Years

At about five years old Ruth is taken to rather swish tea-rooms by her grandparents. Asked what she would like to drink, she replies in a very clear, very loud voice "A hot chocolate please, and I want it now!" The other customers lifted their napkins to cover their faces trying hard not to let Ruth or her embarrassed grandparents see that they are struggling not to laugh.

At twelve years old, Ruth is invited to her great-grandfather's 85th birthday celebration, along with her father and his partner. Also there are Ruth's mother and her husband, together with their son William, Ruth's half brother. Many other relatives also present make it a proper family gathering. The venue is a quaint countryside tea garden, 1920's style. (Unfortunately it closed ten years ago when the owner retired).

That day on the menu: are Home-made *Scones with Jam and Cream*, and *Brown bread and boiled eggs "As you like them"*. The whole ambience is absolutely charming. However, the tables and chairs are very old and quite rickety. This means that everyone has to sit still and not take liberties with the furniture.

With the meal completed the adults begin to talk, catching up on family news. Sitting still and behaving themselves are not really any child's strong point. Ruth and her half brother become bored amongst so many chattering grown-ups. They notice that at one end of the large lawn there is a wooden building with a railed veranda, similar to a village cricket pavilion It was once a beautiful white colour with green rails and fascia board, but now looks rather seedy, the paint has peeled and the wood decayed. Running over to the building the two children begin to enjoy a game of hide and seek. "It's nice to see them play together" says great grandfather. Suddenly there's a loud scream then giggles from Ruth as William disappears through the floor of the veranda. The whole family rush over expecting the worst, William's head is just above the level of the floor. He looks like a loose head from a French guillotine. Like Ruth he's giggling too, although his leg is badly scraped and hurts. The family didn't have to pay for the damage.

The Teens

Ruth was a 'normal' teenager. Her hair was sometimes bright ginger, sometimes purple, sometimes black, sometimes a mixture. it could be medium length, or short and spiky. She wore a nose stud and her ears were pierced in several places. Nothing out of the ordinary there then.

At fifteen Ruth has a paper round. To everyone's surprise takes her work seriously. She's conscientious and quick, never puts a paper through the door of someone who is away on holiday and her collected money is always correct. Some of the boys who work at the newsagents are jealous. So one day they throw her bright yellow newspaper satchel into a skip. Luckily she has finished her round and the satchel is empty. Ruth's not one to cry or be easily defeated. Searching round, she finds an old car wheel and props it against the front of the skip. Using that as a step she climbs into the skip. She slips, legs in the air and knickers showing she overbalances and slides head first down the sloping edge of the skip. Having retrieved the bag she turns round to find that it's a very deep skip and very, very empty. After shouting for help and getting no response, Ruth realises the seriousness of her situation. It takes several attempts before she manages to hook the handle of her satchel onto the projection on the outside of the skip and is able to haul herself out. She later admits to being quite resigned to spending the night in that skip!

Early Adulthood

In her late teens Ruth has a more serious and responsible outlook.

She earns a living serving behind a bar, waitressing, and finally has a job as a shop assistant. She met many types of people and gained a practical knowledge of how the world really works. Deciding she should buckle down and have a proper career, Emily enters university to take a course in dramatic art.

As drama student in her second year at university, Ruth attends a party with her boyfriend Mike. It is a good party and both are rather merry as they wend their way homewards. On the walk home she has to 'spend a penny' and goes behind some bushes in the park. Mike continues on his way, oblivious of her absence. Ruth emerges to find she is alone. Walking along the pavement presents only a minor problem to her as she weaves slightly from side to side taking care not to tread on the cracks between the paving slabs. She realises that eventually she'll need to cross the road to get home and although slightly drunk, walks until she reaches the security offered by a pedestrian crossing. She steps onto it and an approaching car stops. Safely on the other side she ponders the situation with the profound thought processes of the inebriated. Waiting until another car is in sight she crosses back and again the car stops for her. She carries on like this for about ten minutes. Eventually a police car approaches and she steps out again, it waits while she crosses. Some minutes later having completed its patrol of the area the police car returns. Again Ruth steps onto the crossing but now when the car stops one of the policeman steps out to have a quiet word. Ruth does not take kindly to being advised to go home. "I'm an actress" she states firmly, "and I'm creating. I'm creating a live happening" "Look miss, if you don't go home we'll have to take you in".

Later at the police station, the sergeant tries to telephone Mike at the flat—but gets no reply. Ruth refuses to give her father's number, knowing that he'll let her stew in her own juice anyway and later would never forgive her for having him woken at some ungodly hour. Becoming more and more angry at the phone calls being ignored by her boyfriend, and being refused a taxi by the police, Ruth eventually is relieved of her money and belongings and put into a cell for her own good. It turns out that Mike had arrived at the flat and crashed out. It is not until he gets up to answer the phone after daylight that he realises she isn't there.

The Adult World of Work

After gaining her degree Ruth becomes a drama teacher.

Besides producing the end of term shows written and acted by her students she maintains a personal practical outlook by taking the occasional small role in television plays and films.

Last year Ruth and Mike attended a puppetry course in Prague. They now write and give amazing shows at folk festivals in the UK and on the Continent. Mike's occupation as model maker and props maker for films is a great asset.

The Future

Early next Spring, Ruth (now 29), and Mike (32) are getting married; it is sure to be an interesting wedding, the reception is on a large decorated riverboat. I'm looking forward to being there.

A H Tucker (b.1935)

Sad Story

February 1952

It was a cold, dry, Tuesday morning. The bitter east wind snapped at seven-year-old Edwin's legs, chilling the exposed flesh from the top of his calf-length woollen stockings up to where his thighs disappeared into his short, grey-flannel trousers.

Edwin hadn't wanted to go to school that morning. He would have preferred to have stayed tucked-up in bed, peeping from beneath his eiderdown quilt at Jack Frost's artwork on the window-panes; but his pleas of insufferable stomach pains had fallen upon deaf ears.

As he trudged along the frosty pavements with his hands thrust deep into his trouser pockets and his shoulders hunched to protect the back of his neck against the wind's cruel bite, his thoughts were fixed on the day's one saving grace. It was the day his class listened to "Story Time" on the school wireless – his favourite lesson of the week – during the period preceding dinner time.

The early part of the morning dragged for Edwin. He couldn't concentrate on his lessons; his thoughts were preoccupied with "Story Time". 11.30 couldn't come soon enough.

Edwin's form teacher, Miss Fisher, ushered her class into the assembly hall at 11.25. She instructed the children to settle themselves down on the hall's parquet floor as quickly and quietly as possible.

When they were all seated cross-legged in front of the assembly hall stage, Miss Fisher held her open arms high above her head, commanding absolute silence before she would consent to switch on the school wireless.

The school wireless was a dusty old radio receiver, situated on a small table beneath the tall windows at the back of the stage. The receiver was connected to a single speaker, which was housed in a varnished plywood cabinet at the front right-hand side of the stage.

When Miss Fisher switched on the wireless the speaker began to buzz and hum, and emit its familiar ear-piercing noises as the valves in the receiver went through their obligatory warming-up exercises.

Edwin realised there was something wrong straight away. Instead of the cheerful voice of the woman announcer who introduced "Story Time" each week, the first voice to come out of the speaker was that of a very sombre male announcer. In extremely reverential tones the voice informed its audience that His Majesty King George the Sixth had passed away in his sleep during the previous night. The voice went on to announce that all the schools' programmes scheduled for the rest of the day had been cancelled, and would be replaced by music appropriate to the solemnity of the occasion.

Miss Fisher switched off the wireless thirty seconds or so into the string quartet's monotonous dirge. Standing front-centre stage, she told the class that they would have to sit in silence for the remainder of the period as a mark of respect for His Majesty.

The only sounds to enter Edwin's ears were those made by the dinner ladies as they began to set up their trestle-tables at the far end of the hall. Edwin found the silence abominable; shivering on the cold parquet floor, it wasn't long before he began to brood. He felt cheated – after all, he had been wound up all morning, clinging to the promise of a good story. After a short spell of churlish bickering – apportioning blame and formulating suitable punishment – his thoughts turned to the tragic event that had been the root cause of his disappointment. He lingered for a while on the circumstances of His Majesty's demise, '....passed away peacefully in his sleep...', before he found his thoughts drawn to the broader perspective of death itself. His face turned as ashen as the bleak February sky beyond the tall windows at the back of the assembly hall as the full force of his deliberations hit home: 'If it got him, what chance have I got?'

Michael Rowe (b.1945)

Scars

Morning 2.am...

Never had I felt so alone, waiting for him to come for me – waiting for him to tell me he loved me...

It had rained, so as I walked out of the back door of our flat, I noticed water droplets on the hedge which sparkled like diamonds. I heard the engine of his motor bike as he came near. He sped around the corner and stopped – that's when I ran to meet the bike.

'Is that all you're bringing, Babe?' he called. His face dimpled. He looked like a Hell's Angel, only smaller, and of course Ben didn't drink, so I knew it was OK.

'I'm only running away for a week,' I said, alarmed.

He looked me up and down, smiling as his glance came up. 'Nice,' he said in his cheeky way. I was wearing my denim jeans shorts and feeder hoodie with my hair in a loose pony-tail.

'Are you sure you wanna do this?' he asked, as I pulled my leg over the back of his new Harley.

'Of course I am,' I said with some boldness I didn't really feel.

An hour away on the A1, with my arms around his waist, I felt just as sure as rain is wet.

Then it happened – CRASH – BOOM! We were hit by a car...
***

I woke up and realised it had just been a dream. The past now seems clear – just a memory of when Ben and I were the hottest couple in Kenton High School. I feel down my leg. It's still there.

The scars of yesterday...

Ami Gray (b.1990)

School Bully

It was 1956 when I met Mary.

Both shy, awkward loners, we took to each other at once, and quickly discovered, to our mutual delight that we had been born on the same day, and almost at the same hour. We decided then and there that we were twins, and even tried to dress alike. This was easy enough in school uniform, but it was more difficult to persuade our mothers to buy us similar clothes for out-of-school.

Mary insisted that we looked alike. I thought this was wishful thinking. Although we both had brown hair in pigtails, mine was a dark, rich brown, whereas hers was that lighter colour, unkindly known as 'mouse'.

We both had blue eyes. But I argued again. Mary's were truest, deepest blue, like a pre-dawn sky. My eyes are not really blue at all - more a dark, bluish kind of grey.

'Air force blue,' she insisted. And so I acquiesced.

We hated being girls and wished we were boys; we longed to have our hair cut short like "George" in Enid Blyton's Famous Five, but neither set of parents would allow it. And so we had to put up with our pigtails, an ever-present temptation for boys to pull.

Mary and I became inseparable, although we could not sit together in class. She had to sit near the front due to poor hearing, and I had to sit at the back as I was one of the tallest in class. My desk-mate was Joe Warner, a fat boy who always had a snot-nose. He constantly copied my work, but I didn't mind this too much. At least he didn't pull my pigtails or put spiders in my desk, like some boys would have. I frequently lent him handkerchiefs which his mother never washed and returned, until my mum began to complain about the amount of hankies I lost at school. But anything was better than listening to his sniffles and snorts all day. Aside from that, we got along okay.

Years later, I met Joe again at the youth club. He had slimmed down a lot and looked amazingly cool. He told me, among other things, that I had been the only girl in school who had ever been civil to him. Loneliness is more widespread than we imagine.

But every playtime was shared with Mary, and our play was not the usual girlie stuff. We enacted Enid Blyton stories, or favourite historic scenes, invented spooky games and scared ourselves silly; but our favourite game was "stone-agers" when we imagined ourselves as cavemen. Mary shared my fascination for pre-history. Then we began to play a more serious game which we called "Operation Escape". This was because of Shelagh Durran who was the female version of the school bully. I can still recall her dreaded face with clarity. She had thick, ginger-brown hair, coiled into many ringlets which reminded me of sausages. Her eyes were green, slanted, and mocking. She was bigger than the average ten-year-old; not fat, but heftily built. She must have weighed seven stone to my six.

Shelagh had always taken great delight in tormenting Mary. Now she had two of us - quiet girls who wouldn't say "boo" to the proverbial goose. She revelled in the task of making our lives a misery. She was strong, and could twist your arm behind your back until you yelped. She pulled hair much more viciously than the boys ever did - great handfuls of it. I think even they (the boys) were afraid of her.

With the greatest of ease, Shelagh extorted all our pocket money, which was little enough. I got only tuppence a day, and Mary got sixpence as her parents were better off. All this was handed over to Shelagh every morning at break time for "protection" which meant she would beat us up otherwise. I only wish I could have seen through her from the start. It would have saved a lot of trouble for Mary and me.

On one occasion, Shelagh deliberately spilled water on the bench in the art room, just as I was about to sit there. When I had done so and discovered myself to be soaking wet, she promptly wailed to the teacher, 'Please Miss, Bernadette's wet herself!' And she managed to sound genuinely disgusted. I was ordered from the room in disgrace, accompanied by the derision of the class. That was the most humiliating thing she did, but there were many others. Yet it never occurred to us to report Shelagh's misdeeds to a teacher. There was a kind of unwritten law that simply forbade such a thing. To split on a schoolmate was the lowest thing to do. The fact that Shelagh herself did not observe this rule made no difference. Just because she was low didn't mean we had to join her. It was a kind of fierce, unreasoning pride.

There was the time Shelagh ruined Mary's new cardigan. This happened in sewing class. She slyly cut a small piece from Mary's elbow with her scissors, causing a mass of ladders to run straight up the sleeve. Mary was quite distraught when she told me about it. Her mum was likely to hit the roof when she got home. 'Shelagh's a puckfig!' she said with vehemence.

'Oh Mary,' I feigned horror, 'what would your dad say if he heard you say that?'

She grinned. 'He'd probably wash my mouth out with soap. What would your dad say?'

My mind boggled at the thought. 'I bet I wouldn't have a mouth left. I'd still be spitting out teeth.' We lapsed into helpless giggles; and from that day on, Shelagh was referred to as "Puckfig".

So that's what we were up against.

Mary and I began to slip out of school at dinner time to avoid Shelagh. This was against the rules, and we'd have been in trouble if we'd been caught, but we considered it worth the risk. We even gave up having school dinner to avoid seeing her in the dining hall. Hunger was the worst part of this idea and we couldn't use our dinner money to buy food, as this was collected by Miss Benson each Monday morning, which was just as well, else Shelagh would surely have claimed it. We tried to bring extra sandwiches from home for the morning break, without arousing parent's suspicions. These combined with bottles of school milk had to suffice for the day.

Most days we went to the local park. This was about five minute's walk from the rear gate of the school, comprised extensive lawns and gardens, a children's playground, and was situated by the busy River Thames.

We would stand by the waterside railings and watch the little tugs towing barges, while the black oily water made rainbowed slicks along the muddy shore. We loved to see the really big ships which often passed, moving towards Tower Bridge and the Pool of London. These would blow a deafening signal, and the famous bridge would open to allow passage.

Or we might go to the children's playground. Except for a few young mums with toddlers, this would be blissfully deserted on schooldays. As we played on the swings or roundabouts, we would devise elaborate plans for getting rid of Shelagh, none of which we would ever have dared to execute. That's why we called it "Operation Escape".

Although we were heartily ashamed of being so firmly in the power of such a bully, there did not seem to be a way out. If we ganged up on her, she would not hesitate to split on us, then we would be in big trouble – not only at school – our parents would be told. Mary's father was strict, but my stepfather was downright scary. He needed very little excuse to tan my backside with his leather belt. This always happened in the evenings when my mum worked part-time, and the significance of that did not strike me until much later. I just lived in mortal fear of him, and would rather have put up with Shelagh forever than face his anger.

Then came the day she was waiting for us at the school gate, wearing a triumphant grin on her freckled face. 'Where have you been?' she wanted to know. 'Tell me, or I'll split!'

Mary was quicker-witted than I. She tipped me a blue-eyed wink and nudged me to silence. 'We've been to explore the bommies,' she lied.

The bommies were derelict bombed houses, of which there were an abundance in the East End. These were considered unsafe and definitely out of bounds for schoolchildren.

156

Shelagh's green eyes gleamed wickedly. 'I'm gonna split,' she announced.

I summoned courage. 'That's 'cos you wouldn't dare go there. They're haunted, you know.'

'Pah!' she exclaimed. 'There ain't no such thing as ghosts!'

But we could see her pride was rankled. The bell sounded at that moment and she viciously yanked a pigtail from each of us, almost knocking our heads together.

Mary and I were on tenterhooks all afternoon, expecting Shelagh to split, but amazingly, she didn't. I thought she must have something else in mind, and I was right.

School broke out at 4.30.p.m. and I had a fairly long walk home. On wintry evenings, I usually made it just before full darkness, which was when my parents expected me. I was naturally dismayed when Shelagh began to walk with me. It was not her usual direction and I did not relish the thought of her company.

'Show me these bommies,' she commanded.

'It'll be dark soon,' I protested.

'Who's scared now?' she jeered.

'Okay Shelagh.' And I led her to the eeriest derelict I knew – Spinner's Haunt.

Spinner's Haunt was a particular bombed house which appeared to have been cleaved straight down the middle, and was still attached to the end of an abandoned terrace. It was spooky to see half a house like that. The place whispered of death and destruction, and fired the imagination. Mary and I had made up our own story about it, just the way we made up stories about everything.

Mildewed wallpaper still clung to the standing walls, and two black fireplaces resembled open yawning mouths in the fading light. The staircase was miraculously intact, though it swayed and groaned as if tired of waiting for demolition. The roof was gone, but the one of the adjoining house could be reached from the upper level, via broken brickwork which had formed convenient steps in the rear wall.

Shelagh gripped my arm with a heavy hand. 'Why is it called Spinner's Haunt?'

I could see she was scared; the atmosphere was getting to her. 'Spinner was the dog who used to live here,' I lied in a whispering voice. 'He was killed when the house was bombed, along with all of the children. He still comes back to look for them. After dark, if you sit on the roof, you can hear him howling. It's really very sad. Mary and me have heard him.'

'You've sat on the roof?' She looked incredulous and eyed the creaking staircase with apprehension.

'Yeah, you can't hear him otherwise,' I reminded.

'Then I'm gonna do it!' she said defiantly. 'I'll show you who's a scaredy-cat.' She glared at me, green eyes more feline than she knew.

'You'll have to go first, to show me the way.'

'Okay,' I said with less hesitation than I felt. I'd often made this climb before, though never in growing darkness. Still, I was more scared of Shelagh than I was of the dark. My heart hammered in my chest, but I wasn't going to chicken out now.

I began to climb the creaky staircase. That was the easy bit. Shelagh followed, gripping the banister for support, careful not to let me out of her sight. We reached the upper level, and stood precariously in the remains of a bedroom. 'Mind the hole in the floor,' I warned. 'Walk around the edge like me.'

She nodded, too fearful to notice who was giving the orders. We reached the stepped brickwork. I was just as scared as she was, but for a different reason. I wondered if she would push me off the roof. Was she capable of murder? Or she might do it in a moment of panic. Either way, I didn't trust her one little bit. Alone on a roof with Shelagh was the last place in the world I wanted to be.

I reached the top and stood on a ledge which must have once been part of the chimney stack. Shelagh arrived to join me, panting as much from fear as physical effort. The black-tiled roof of the next house reached about waist level, and stretched before us, resembling a pyramid in the half-light. Stars had begun to wink, and cold wind whistled past our ears. 'You've gotta ride the roof,' I wickedly informed.

She gulped and visibly paled in the starlight. 'Go on then, Bernie Big-head,' she taunted. 'You go first.'

There didn't seem to be much choice. I hoisted myself to the apex of the sloping roof and sat astride. Then I made my way to the middle, shifting my weight alternately from hands to thighs. The slates were icily cold and damp, like gravestones, I thought. Mary and I, or street mates usually did this daredevil feat in the summer when the black-tiled roofs were warm. What happens to the blatant nerve of the very young? I could never attempt such a thing now. I did not even think to glance down at the drop to the street below. It never occurred to me that I might fall, unless Shelagh had any thing to do with it.

I half-turned, twisting my body to look back at her. 'Come on, Shelagh,' I coaxed. 'It's good up here.' I could see she was petrified, and obviously had no head for heights, yet determined not to lose face. She placed her hands on the crest of the roof, and I turned away to hide my grinning face.

Then somewhere not too distant, a dog howled mournfully in the silent night. This could not have been better timed if I had arranged it. And it was more than enough for Shelagh. She screamed and fled. I heard her frantic footsteps descending the brickwork, and then the staircase, then all was silent; she'd bottled out. I threw back my head and laughed aloud at the twinkling stars. 'Thanks, Spinner old mate!' I yelled. Serves you right, Puckfig! I thought savagely to Shelagh.

A moment of short-lived glory.

Her revenge would be swift and sure.

Bernie Morris

School Fight

South Manchester High School was split into two locations, which only meant that the grimness and decay was doubled. I spent the majority of my time at the south campus where the only redeeming features were my gorgeous classmates, Shirley Granby and Melanie Wall, as well as that rare thing – a decent teacher: two, in fact, Mrs Armstrong and Mr Pugh. Mr Pugh was the PE teacher who tried his best to motivate us to get fit, and wasn't shy with the strap on the hand when faced with misbehaviour. The one occasion when I attracted his displeasure was by kicking a football inside the changing room which broke a light. Surprisingly, in his office, he only told me not to do it again. Years after school I found out my grandmother's maiden name was Pugh, so I like to think he sensed a family connection there between us.

For some reason the powers that be made my Year spend a couple of terms up at the north campus. And what a dilapidated and depressing toilet that was. The day that stands out most for me during my school days happened there. I was standing watching a football game under one of those covered walkways. Suddenly, without warning, I was punched high on the right side of my face. I knew it was a left handed punch. My best mate, Stuart, was a leftie. Imagine my surprise when I realised it was him punching me. I was too stunned to think about defending myself. I just asked him why he had done that. His reason was that I had continually told my family to tell him, either on the phone or at the door, that I was out. In a split second I thought of my recent actions; maybe I had been busy with a project, or with my hobby of snooker. Also in that short time I could see the gang of lads behind Stuart – his friends from one of his own interest groups. Thinking about it later, I had subconsciously seen them circling me, of course without knowing why. Perhaps egged on from behind, Stuart punched me again. Now I responded, throwing a punch and then getting involved in some grappling. I was hit badly again. I managed a great left hook (which in truth was probably a flailing swing) which connected with his right eyebrow, cutting it. I also came up with a right uppercut which almost broke his teeth. I remember the sound of his jaw slamming shut to this day. But, basically, I got beaten up.

It was over quite quickly. I was left to nurse my wounds while the group dispersed. Some other pupils had witnessed it, and also two of the less caring teachers who had no intention of disturbing their cigarette break to run over and stop a fight. Grange Hill this place certainly wasn't.

Stuart and I never spoke again. From time to time, as adults, our paths crossed. I've only ever glanced at him. I like to think his reserved manner near me is through long-held guilt or regret. I've never considered any kind of revenge. I probably never will, unless we both find ourselves eventually in the old people's home which was built on the demolished north campus.

GB Hope (b.1970)

Seven Jumpers

I was born during a snowstorm, so I've been told, and have been uncommonly sensitive to cold ever since.

When I was just eighteen months old, my little brother Jim had the nerve to be born and I was immediately upgraded (if you can call it that) to the "pram seat", perched above the tiny baby in the pram whenever Mum took us out. I did not like this promotion at all. Suddenly I was exposed to the elements without blankets or protective pram hood. I felt every gust of wind, flake of snow and nip of frost. Even though Mum always wrapped me up warmly, with coat, two bonnets, double mittens and scarf, still after being out for more than ten minutes, I would begin to cry with the cold, so we'd have to turn around and go home again.

One of my worst memories is of the time my mum took my older brother, Richard, fishing. She knew absolutely nothing about fishing and neither did he, but they'd improvised with a home-made rod and line, a safety pin on the end, and a few worms they'd dug up. It was around March and not particularly cold, but blustery enough for little old me. I remember their comments that there were loads of tiny fish nibbling at the bait, but none too daft to be caught. In the meantime, I was stuck in the push-chair, waiting patiently and freezing my socks off, until I began to howl in protest. So guess what? We had to go home again with Richard grumbling all the way about what a sissy wuss his little sister was. After that I think Mum bought him a long-handled net to catch small fry with.

When I was about three or four, we moved from the flat into our first house in a quiet road. That was pleasant enough as there was a huge hedge of blue hydrangea in the front garden and an apple tree and a swing out the back. I got to have my own bedroom for the first time ever, which was just a box room and about the same size as one – just big enough to hold my two-foot bed and a toy box. I can remember my mum painting the door and window frame in pink gloss, just for me.

Yes, it was lovely at first with the sun streaming through my front window every morning. But then the winter arrived. Very few houses had central heating then, and those that did could hardly afford to run it. Ours didn't have it. My family, skint as ever, could only afford two paraffin heaters downstairs and one in the bathroom, and these were lit only one at a time, depending on which room you were in.

Quite often, about halfway through the week, Mum's money would run out, or at least be prioritised for food and rent, so there would be no more paraffin until pay day. On these occasions, we would be sent to bed early, just to keep warm. I can remember snuggling into my blankets and watching my breath turning to ice on the window. I would imagine myself as the Snow Queen, able to freeze everything I touched.

Several years later, in yet another house, when my youngest brother, Lawrence was less than a year old, and I was about seven or eight, we had our gas supply cut off due to non payment – and that was the coldest winter ever. These days, I don't think it would be allowed, not with a baby and four other children in the family. At first, there was no heat in the house at all, except for an upright paraffin stove which was also used to boil the kettle on top. But then the social service helped out a bit by providing us with an electric hotplate for cooking, and a fan heater which could be moved from room to room. Luckily, we still had an immersion heater for hot water, so we sort-of managed without gas for eighteen months or so, until my mum had saved enough money to pay off the bill.

You see, there was no credit back then, if you couldn't pay, you didn't get; it was normal practice. I can remember waking up in the morning and mentally steeling myself to get out of bed and confront the icy atmosphere – that you could see yourself breathing as if you were smoking a cigarette. I can remember that there was ice on the windows making pretty patterns – inside. I no longer imagined myself as the

Snow Queen, rather a victim of the fabled Jack Frost. I took to wearing my coat indoors, and got away with this by telling everyone it was my makeshift dressing-gown. My mum sympathised, as she knew I was more susceptible to the cold than most. My brothers just laughed; I guess they were more inured to it than me.

I developed a routine of morning dressing. I would sit up in bed and reach out to my chest-of-drawers before getting out. I would put several items on before braving the elements and throwing back the duvet, then I would quickly don tights and trousers. On one such morning, I emerged into the kitchen with my coat already on. My mum always made us delicious creamy porridge in the winter months, and mine was rapidly cooling on the table. She said, 'I know you're a bit late, dear,' without really looking at me. So I wolfed it down and made my escape.

When I got to school and took my coat off, my teacher looked at me aghast and said, 'My God, Jane, are you putting on weight?'

You see, I was wearing seven jumpers, one on top of the other.

Janie Quittenton b.1968

She Made a Difference

(Referring to a dedicated childcare manager)

She said she cared so much because she was the one who'd "caught me flying through the door", but I think every one of us kids in care was special to her in some way or another. Bernie had that knack of making you feel like you belonged and were wanted. Even though she was a shorty and round, with her flaming red hair and piercing eyes she was not to be messed with. What Bernie said went and she would take on anyone, no matter how big or scary, to ensure that we were okay. It didn't matter who she upset along the way. I remember hearing that once a woman jumped over a sofa and bolted out of the door because Bernie pointed out the facts to her.

To me, Bernie had an amazing presence; when she walked in a room and spoke, it was something worth listening to and taking note of. I remember once when Jo and I were going out to meet some boys in the park, all dressed up with loads of make-up on. She was standing at the bottom of the stairs by the office door, arms crossed over her ample bosom and just telling us in her broad Irish accent to "get our arses back upstairs and take that shite off our faces". We used to moan and call her an old witch – and worse! But really we were secretly glad that someone cared enough to tell us off.

She had a good heart and would always listen to what I had to say. I would sit in her office talking about anything and everything, knowing that at last someone understood. At fourteen that's important. I was so lucky as things could have easily been so different.

With Bernie's support I felt like anything was possible; all my hopes, dreams and ambitions really could come true. I was capable of anything if I just put my mind to it.

Bernie was truly amazing. It wasn't just us though; she had looked after many different kids for the last twenty-five years as well as bringing up her own daughter by herself.

She once told me that she would continue to do so as long as she could make a difference. Unfortunately, the system finally started failing and letting the kids down and she, in turn, no longer felt that such a difference was possible.

The things Bernie said and did I will never forget. (I even use some of her quotes myself now!) She taught me how to love and be loved, to trust and be trusted, and most of all that it was all right to be myself and that I was safe and nobody could ever hurt me again. It is because of Bernie that I am who I am today – a person I actually like, and for that I thank her from the bottom of my heart.

Lindsey Golightly (b.1979)

She Threw the Book at Me

I was educated in Ireland in the early thirties, and in those days there wasn't much choice; you learned the three R's and that was it. No further education was available unless you were considered brainy enough to go to college.

So I was in the top class at age thirteen – had been there for the past year, going over and over the same curriculum. My teacher was Miss Denny, a formidable tartar. My mother, who hated me anyway, had once told me that she had learned under Miss Denny, and that if you could pass her class, you could do anything.

I can't remember what I did wrong on this occasion; I think I might have been talking in class, and that when Miss Denny challenged me, I must have given her some kind of back-chat. I guess I always opened my mouth and put my foot in it, as that was my way. Anyway, she was so mad that she literally threw a book at me that hit me on the nose and close to the eye. I almost passed out with the impact, but somehow managed not to. I think my nose bled a bit too.

That afternoon when I got home, my mother asked me if I'd been fighting. I truthfully said "no" and went to bed early after doing my usual household chores.

The next morning I looked in the mirror and gasped to see that I had a real black "shiner" and that half of my face was swollen up, including my nose. I looked like a monster. I hardly dared to go downstairs for breakfast, which I usually made, but was soon alerted by my mother's calling, 'Git yer lazy arse down here!'

I tried to look inconspicuous, but of course she noticed my face. 'What the hell happened to you?' she asked.

'Oh, I fell and hit a wall,' I told her.

'Typical clumsy eejit!' she said.

The next day a friendly neighbour asked her, 'What are you going to do about your poor Nellie's face? If that were me, I'd be straight up to see the teacher.'

My mum thought about this, then marched to the school to meet Miss Denny. Once she'd heard her story she was down on me like a ton of bricks, not only for talking in class and giving cheek to the teacher, but also for telling lies and making her look a fool.

I guess I couldn't win whatever I did.

Ellen Bennett (b. 1919)

Shooting Star

This was my one moment of absolute glory – my first and last opportunity to "shine".

I was six years old and the school was rehearsing for the Christmas play. Gail Belcher was to have the starring role as Fairy Queen, as she had long blonde hair right down to her bottom.

I was originally cast as a "bouncing ball". It was the story of a toyshop where all the toys magically came to life. I wasn't particularly enamoured of this role, as it felt rather silly to keep jumping up and down at rehearsals; but I had no words to say and was determined to give it my best shot. At least I wasn't a "spinning top" which would have been far more uncomfortable. The boy who had this part kept falling over on stage, but that was considered OK, as that's what spinning tops eventually do.

But then, two days before the grand event, Gail was taken ill with the flu' and was off school. I guess the teachers panicked. I was immediately selected as stand-in, even though I wasn't half as pretty as Gail, and because I knew the lines. I had long hair, normally worn in pigtails, but although it had started off blonde in my first three years, it had now darkened to chestnut brown. However, I tried on the white, sparkly dress and it fitted perfectly. I guess I was the natural choice.

I remember my first night of stardom, as I wasn't the least bit shy then. I stood in centre stage and spouted these words:

I am the Fairy Queen
This is the toyshop
I shall wave my magic wand
And all the toys will come to life
Then we shall have some fun.

I then skipped around the stage, pointing the said wand at all and sundry. I don't remember much more about the event, except it was a howling success and the audience cheered so much.

I had to perform this three times more for various parents and schoolmates who were unable to attend the first night. I didn't mind this at all. For the first time in my life – I was a star.

Bernie Morris

Silly Moo

Once on a holiday to Buncrana when I was very young, we went to visit an uncle who lived on his own in a big farmhouse. It was nice and cosy, sitting around the old range. My dad and uncle started telling us stories about when they were younger, and the things they got up to, and also tales of the spooky kind. Because I was so young, these spooky stories scared me, (literally scared the shit out of me).

So I needed to go to the little girls' room and my uncle's farmhouse, like many other ancient buildings, didn't have a little girls' room and the outside toilet was right down the end of a long yard. But I desperately needed to go, so my dad discreetly asked what I wanted to "do".

I said I just needed a wee, so my uncle said, 'Just go in the barn outside there now, Caroline, and you can pee to your hearts content'.

I asked and prayed for my sister to come out there with me, as even though this was closer to the house, I still didn't like the dark, but there was no persuading her at all. She wanted to hear more spooky stories, so as nature was getting the better of me, I had to go alone.   I ran into the barn as quickly as my little legs were able to carry me. Down came the knickers in the darkness, and then I saw two glowing eyes, and I heard it: "MOOO..."

Jeez – I never stopped to pick up the knickers, but ran faster back to the house, than I'd ever got out there. I was as white as a ghost, and when I eventually told them what I was blubbering about, they all laughed their socks off. But God-bless Uncle, he found more than he'd bargained for when he went to "muck-out" in the morning.

A couple of days later, we were on the farm again. My uncle wanted to move the cows from one field to another, so he told me to stand at the end of the lane, with arms stretched wide just in case one took a detour. He knew by now I was a bit scared of cows, so he told me, 'Now don't worry about the cows, Carol, they are more afraid of you than you of them, but if they should come your way, just clap your hands and shoo them back, but sure you'll have nothing to worry about, they won't come near you at all.'

Guess what? Sure enough, one came ambling towards me. I clapped my hands. She said, 'MOOO,' and I ran like the clappers. The cow got loose, and so the rest of the herd followed her down the lane, with a not-too-pleased uncle giving chase.

Caroline Morgan (b.1955)

Smoking in the 60s

Everyone did it. I guess in the Fifties we all thought of it as a grown-up thing. Mum and Dad did it, aunties and uncles too. Teachers and policemen did it. Doctors did it – and even the parish priest did it. It was just a normal thing to us kids – some sort-of grown-up ritual, which we didn't even bother to think about, because it didn't affect us in any way at all. It was even advertised on telly as being "good for you". Sometimes I think we "baby boomers" ought to sue the government for that kind of brainwashing.

But I honestly can't remember ever being bothered by such a thing as "passive smoking"; there again, I guess I was inured to it. I was raised in the London smogs of the Fifties, so I would imagine that cigarette smoke was nothing by comparison.

I remember one winter's evening when I was about fifteen, going out to choir practice at the local church. It was a thick pea-souper, and you literally couldn't see your hand in front of your face, so I kept my scarf over my mouth and just felt my way there along the railings and walls. What should have been a ten-minute walk actually took me twenty.

The parish priest had the cheek to ask me why I was late, so I didn't bother to tell him that I wasn't going to come any more. If he didn't know why I was late, he could do the other thing after I'd made so much effort to get there. He then had the audacity to light up a fag during tea-break, right there in church! He even used one of the blessed candles to do it. All of us kids excused this at the time, on the grounds that he was a priest and therefore holy and righteous. What brainwashed eejits we were!

I got home that night and looked in the mirror with shock. My blonde hair had turned to charcoal-grey. That's how much shite was in the London smog – and that's how much dirt must have been in my lungs. My Mum and Dad were still smoking in front of the telly and the coal fire was burning merrily, unwittingly adding to the black cloud over the city.

I joined them gratefully.

Bernie Morris b. 1946

Snow Bear

Way back in 1933 when I was twelve years old, we were living in a small Cumbrian town situated some nine miles east of Carlisle and, as usual, winter was winter, Cumbrian style.

At the time of the occasion about to be revealed there was much snow about and continuing awful – not that I minded, I loved it – heavy, sleeting snow driven by a fair wind and "cold with it". I carried my home-made sledge up the tiring road to the big field belonging to a local farmer. There I joined a number of other kids who were already enjoying themselves with their sledges of various shapes and sizes, struggling up a long, steep slope that was deeply covered in crispy-topped snow, to throw themselves into the serious business of sliding at some speed down the incline.

It was late afternoon and after some time, many of the other boys started to leave, going home for tea, I suppose. But I continued in my activity because it was a serious business to me. I was in the Yukon! I knew all about the Yukon, Alaska and the Mackenzie Territory, because for about two years I had buried myself in every book I could find on the North West: peoples, history, seasons, gold-mining, trapping, hunting, wildlife on the land and in the sea as well as the lakes and rivers – and the Malemutes pulling loaded dog sledges. Ah, the wonder of it all!

One school teacher said to me one day, 'Boy, I do believe you will end up writing books about Canada and Alaska, but don't forget the other parts of the world.'

Anyway, time passed and I was left alone in the gathering gloom, buried in my thoughts, struggling up the hill and careering down it, despite the increase in wind and tormenting sleet that was becoming quite fierce. I couldn't see very far because the only light was coming from the the snow and that appeared grey.

Then I heard a roaring sound and stood awhile, listening... Again! A horrible roaring, a bear! It must be, but where? I peered into the sleeting snow. Ah! There – a huge creature – must be a grizzly, moving heavily towards me. What now? What to do?

'Damn it, boy! I'll kill you one of these days!'

FATHER – all six-feet-three of him wrapped up in his thick, snow-covered, Melton overcoat. 'Come on, your mother's going mad. Have you no idea of time? God in heaven!'

Then we slipped and slithered our way home.

Leopold Howe (b.1921)

Soldiers on the Ceiling

When I was about five years old, I went down with a childhood ailment: measles. I was quite ill as there was nothing much to combat it in those days. Rather than my mother having to run up to the next floor all day, I was put in my parents' big soft bed on the first floor.

Dad worked shifts as a driver on the GWR so Mum was able to sleep with me as he wasn't there. All the evacuees were up on the next floor so they wouldn't catch the bug.

Mum had lit a coal fire in the grate which was next to the bed and the room was warm and rosy in the gas light and firelight. She had put the old blackened tin kettle on the side of the fire bars and it was steaming gently to vaporise the air. There was a chipped cream enamel wash bowl with a white flannel to help "take down" my temperature when put on my forehead.

The stairs door, next to the bed, led down to the kitchen and sculleries. The house was an old Georgian terrace and leaned crookedly east so none of the doors fitted well and there was an inch gap on the west edge of the doors as they all faced south. This always caused a considerable draught and you could see the flames in the fire flicker sideways in the fire grate.

When my father was in bed he always wore a highly striped, hand-knitted tea cosy as a hat, so his head didn't get the full draught through the bars of the headboard. Looking up I could see it hanging on its usual coat hook on the back of the bedroom door – very comforting to see it there. All this is held softly in my memory as I remember lying ill in bed.

I could feel the damp dark curls stuck around my face, down my neck and on the white flannelette pillowcase. In the distance I could hear, above the steaming kettle, the crackling of the coals and the hissing of the gas light, the faint sound in the distance of a brass band playing. It was slowly coming nearer.

Looking up at the firelit shadows on the ceiling, I saw coming into view, marching massed army guards' bands in full bearskins and red tunics. Not one was more than two or three inches high and they were upside down as though I were looking down on their bearskins instead of up. They stamped over the cobbles with cymbals crashing and drums beating. The sergeant was barking out commands. There they were marching back and forth, turning, wheeling to the music. On they went, I felt, keeping me safe, until I fell into a deep, trouble-free sleep.

Mum told me after, it was all hallucinations brought on by the illness or "upset liver".

Whatever the reason, all I have to do to find comfort, I imagine again going back in time, to remember my Mum's fussing and those massed bands still marching over the ceiling all those years ago.

Colleen Thatcher b.1937

Soot and Sunlight

During WW2 when I was about six years old, my older brothers and sister were doing their bit; one in the Territorial Army, one in the Royal Navy and my sister was a WAF. We had four east-ender evacuees. These were: Reg, aged thirteen (he later became a cartoonist for a national newspaper); his brother Ken, aged about ten; their cousin Teddy was twelve and a girl called Glenda. My two cousins, Rose and Dick, had Peter and John billeted with them.

We had fun in between air raids: staggered school attendances and helping the grown-ups to "make do". This involved helping in the gardens and allotments and, sometimes in the vegetable fields, on a farm about a mile from home.

One warm, sunny day, the boys decided we could help even more by sweeping the chimney as my father would usually do in summer. So as my mother was not home at the time, we got the brushes and rods all together and with a lot of sorting and arguing, got ready to start.

Our house was four storeys high and there were six fireplaces with back dampers to go through from the kitchen, which was the main living room of the house. We needed lots of rods to screw to the big round broom-head. The boys attached them one by one, as they pushed it up the chimney. Of course no-one had thought of covering anything up, but we had taken out the big hand-made rag rug and spread it on the back bricks in the garden. As the boys twisted and pushed, we younger ones ran back and forth down the garden to see if it had reached the top yet. The brush kept getting stuck as it reached a fireplace or a junction. More and more force was needed and even more hands to push it yet higher. It took an awful long time and there was lots of soot floating around. Eventually it popped out with a shower of soot over the dormer window and the skylight in the roof. With a loud cheer we littl'uns ran back in to tell the boys of our triumph.

But getting it all back down again was another matter that no-one had thought of beforehand. It took everyone pulling and twisting to get it even back inside the chimney pot. The rods rattled in the brickwork, and though we didn't know it at the time, these were leaving trails of soot around each fireplace as they were pulled down. The boys were unscrewing the rods as they each appeared in the kitchen fireplace. All in a mess as you can imagine. Suddenly it jammed in the parlour fireplace, on the next floor up. They sent a couple of kids up with rods to push down as they pulled. With a huge wrench it suddenly sprang out of the fireplace with all the previous winter's soot in one big pile. It went everywhere – all over the china on the dresser, the gaslight globe, the chairs, the clean-scrubbed kitchen table, curtains, pictures, mirror mantle and floor. It was floating out of the window and out into the scullery, covering the oven, sink, wainscot and pantry as it went, all just as my mother was returning home.

To say there was a look of horrified amazement on her face was a bit of an understatement. As she came in we were all sprawled over the lino' covered in soot, coughing, spluttering, laughing and gasping for breath. Even Mother had to finally give in, and laugh with us (or maybe cry).

The only cleaning implements in those days were brooms, dustpan and brush, Sunlight soup, hot soda water and scrubbing brushes, with lots of elbow grease involved.

I don't remember, but I expect we had a good fire the following winter. They were still finding soot in strange places well after VJ Day. We weren't ever allowed to forget it, I can tell you, and never dared to offer that sort of help again!

Colleen Thatcher (b.1937)

Stolen Toffees and a Beautiful Teacher

My story is set in 1960 when I was nine years old. Schooldays all those years ago seemed to encapsulate an even mixture of pleasure and pain if the accuracy of the memory banks are to be believed to any degree. This is just one, and the most memorable story of many spent at St Oswald's Junior, Church of England School that I attended from 1955 to 1962.

The School was situated on the border of Collyhurst, North Manchester, just off the A664 Rochdale Road about a mile from the city centre and the main arterial link to Rochdale and Oldham. On the long walk to school I would pass the stone cobbled streets of terraced houses with the obligatory handy corner grocery shops, empty scrubland, main line railways with their clattering, chuffing steam engines that would draw long lines of goods wagons or sleek passenger carriages past the many industrial units and plethora of dismal looking factories that dotted my route. Eventually the tall, imposing, heavy dark stone built Dickensian looking outline of my school and adjoined church with its crooked steeple, loomed up into view, dwarfing the surrounding small houses.

Before entering the school playground, a small corner sweet or 'toffee shop' two streets away provided a safe harbour of wonderment before the day's lessons and those huge navy blue and black painted doors closed behind us.

The sloping counter top was of a height that gave a child's eye level view of well-stocked masses of sugary confectionery. Two pennies would gain you access to: flying saucers, sherbet dabs, liquorice root sticks, aniseed balls, one penny gob-stoppers, sweet cigarettes, jelly babies, arrow bars, cinder toffee, cherry lips, dolly mixtures, humbugs and a thousand other temptations for sweet-toothed children. I think everyone's favourites were the black-jacks and fruit salad, mainly because eight of these could be purchased for just one old penny piece.

That day would be no exception to my regular toffee consumption as I tucked my eight fruit salad and one penny arrow bar in my pocket and entered the school, up the flight of stone steps to the first floor, to my cream and blue painted classroom where the newly purchased toffees were reverently placed in a cardboard box, (standard school issue that also contained our school books), before the desk lid was closed to await our lunch break.

As the headmaster entered the classroom, a deathly hush fell on the pupils. This man commanded immediate and utter respect; he was not to be trifled with and 'ruled with a rod of iron', or more accurately, a heavy leather strap, cut to provide three stinging tails that hung menacingly on display from his right hip.

The headmaster was followed into the room by a young woman. After the morning greetings of "good morning class", followed by the usual drawn out return of "gooood morrrrrniing, Mr Maaatheeer" our new teacher was introduced as Miss Ainsworth. Wow! Even at that tender age we all acknowledged she was an absolute stunner, with the perfect hour glass figure, the tight fitting skirt and top, and the perfectly manicured hair and make up, we instantly fell madly in love with our beautiful new teacher.

A new pupil had been introduced to us at the same time as our new teacher.

The headmaster had explained that 'Kevin' was new to the area and could we please look after him and familiarise Kevin with the school's routine. He was ushered down the rows of desks and found a seat next to me. After the headmaster had left the classroom, we all introduced ourselves to Miss Ainsworth who informed us that she lived with her parents who... wait for it... owned a sweet shop! We were absolutely in awe of her with her radiant beauty and soft soothing voice and... she lived in a sweet shop, the perfect teacher! School days were definitely getting better from here on!

I took Kevin 'under my wing' so to speak as he seemed a retiring, shy sort of boy with nothing much to say.

Kevin hung back in the classroom and didn't join us at playtime. Our little gang of six (me, Philip, Jed, James, Albert and David) decided that come lunchtime we would invite Kevin to join us in our games and to share our toffees.

As lunchtime arrived, I returned the reading books to my desk and searched my box for the toffees... they were gone! I frantically searched the box and my desk once again but all to no avail; my toffees had been stolen!

The rest of the class had left by this time and I joined them in the playground. Feeling thoroughly down in the dumps I reported to my friends what had happened who then proceeded to share their toffees with me. Thefts had never occurred before, so we were a little perturbed but nevertheless were not in a position to point any accusing fingers!

The next day, I kept my toffees in my pocket to be on the safe side, but at lunchtime Albert found to his utter dismay that his precious toffees had mysteriously vanished from his desk.

We had to find out who the toffee thief was and quickly. The obvious choice was Kevin as the disappearing toffee phenomenon had not started until he had joined our class and, as James pointed out, "Why did Kevin stay behind in class at break-time?"

Between ourselves we devised a cunning plan! The toffee wrappers would be marked in some way so if they disappeared again Philip would approach Kevin and strike up a conversation, casually dropping a hint that he was collecting toffee wrappers and did he have any to spare?

The next day we all placed our marked toffees in our desks and applied the devious master plan. At lunchtime, sure enough, toffees were missing from my desk and James's. Kevin fell into the trap, hook, line and sinker when he produced the marked toffee wrappers at Philip's request.

I quickly challenged Kevin who at first denied the dastardly deed then started throwing punches. As the accusations, hair and blood flew and we ended up on the playground floor a heavy hand grabbed me by the collar and hauled me off Kevin then up to the headmaster's office where I received 'six of the best' from the dreaded leather strap, for 'bullying the new lad'.

My friends had not deserted me, however, and had followed on behind pleading my innocence to the headmaster, while trying to explain about the stolen toffees and how we had marked the wrappers.

Of course he didn't listen to a word they said and metered out the unjust and unfair punishment undeterred.

Kevin had been allowed to leave school early that day to avoid any more confrontation between us. I was given a letter to take to my parents which I opened on the way home; all it said was I had been fighting in the playground – nothing else, so I burned it.

A few days later we managed to 'ambush' Kevin on the way home from school; we didn't touch him but explained in no uncertain terms that friends didn't steal from each other and that we would have shared with him anyway had we been given a chance... we then let him go. The damage to his reputation had been done though and no-one wanted to be his friend after that episode.

Miss Ainsworth was a lovely teacher and always found different and interesting ways of teaching class that added lots of variety to our lessons. She seemed to understand what had happened over the toffee fiasco and became more of a friend to me and us kids rather than an authoritarian figure.

After the summer break we returned to school to find we had a new teacher, a Mrs Kirkham... Miss Ainsworth had got married! She hadn't changed though; she was still our lovely teacher.

As Christmas approached I had become ill with the flu so had to have time off school. As I recovered, my mother decided it was not worth me going back for only two days so I could have an extended Christmas break. As I played with my train set in the front room there was a knock on the front door. When I opened the door I got the shock of my life!

There before me stood the other love of my life, a girl from my class. Susan had been the focus from afar for my affections in the last year or so. With lovely long blonde hair woven into perfect plaits framing her beautiful little face she stood there in her flowery yellow dress and white cardigan, white socks and black patent shoes; she looked absolutely gorgeous! As I stood there dumb struck, she held out a box of 'Milk Tray' chocolates. "Mrs Kirkham has sent you these," she informed.

As I reached forward to take the chocolates our hands touched for a fleeting second when time seemed to stand still for an eternity. I managed to stammer, "Thank you Susan," before she pulled back, throwing me a strange look as if I had suddenly grown two heads, before turning on her heels and quickly hurrying away.

That was as close as I got to 'my' Susan as our paths never crossed again. That following summer all us kids sat our eleven plus exam and went our separate ways to secondary or grammar schools.

I often think back to St Oswald's and Mrs Kirkham nee Ainsworth and wonder what happened to her. I hope she had a wonderful life and enjoyed love and happiness with a very special person... I'll never forget how she was a very special teacher to me.

Dave Clarke b.1951

Sunshine

I am sitting, curled up in bed reading a book. Not a specific book, just one picked at random from the many on my shelf. Using the radio as background noise, my foot occasionally tapping to the bass rhythm of a song I register, or laughing out loud to a comment the radio host made. I'm not really thinking about much. Why should I? I'm 18, tired, and have had a bad day at work. Why should I think big thoughts, whilst reading a book picked at random, listening to old music? It's old because I'm 18, because it wasn't recorded in the last few months. In fact it's classic because it was recorded more than five years ago. These songs don't make me think; some of them might remember a time and a place, but I've had a bad day and so I'm not concentrating on them. I'm flicking through my book to one of the better chapters.

Skimming a page and the first strings of the song start playing; my ears pick it up like a satellite, and suddenly I don't really care about the book I wasn't really reading, or that I've had a bad day at work. I let my brain follow the words, let them roll, because even though I can't sing and I'm a little out of tune, I know them off by heart. I let my mind wander to a time and place, so long ago I would term it ancient history in my youthful arrogance. The time was early 90's and the place: a pink bedroom.

It's sunny outside, warmish for an English spring or summer day. I can't really place it; it's a hazy memory. It could even have just been a good autumn day. I was the luckiest little girl in the world, my mother's little sunshine. She had cut her hair before I could remember and had kept it short ever since I could. Pale white skin consumed with freckles, delicate bone structure on a skinny fame. To assume that this woman was, as she seemed, frail and delicate is to assume wrong. This woman, my mother had a legendary temper: one of the only things I inherited from her, for I certainly didn't get the delicate frame, so breakable, ha!

So there we are: her standing in her trade-mark outfit of little t-shirt and shorts that cover a backside that is barely a backside. I would be jealous if it wasn't my mother's behind. What am I saying? Of course I'm jealous.

She's got in her hand, as she stands in front of my wall, a Disney book: Peter Pan. She's studying the cover: the cartoon little boy with his arms flung out, in his green tunic and leggings on a blue background. I'm sitting on the floor a short distance from her, propped up against the built-in wardrobe. With paper strewn around me, childish imitations of the Disney books likewise distributed as the paper. I'm trying to concentrate, but I'm a child 6 or 7 years old and my mother enthrals me with her movements as she picks up the next colour of crayon she's using.

Peter Pan is half done on my wall when suddenly I have to, I just have the urge to; I run up behind her and because I've inherited her height, I hug her around the waist. It's higher than me and I'm on tiptoes, but she just looks down on me and even though I've interrupted her, she's not mad. She just hugs me back and says, "We need a break, I'll make something to eat" or at least that's the gist of what I remember her saying. The song ends and the memory fades, but I close my eyes and smile, sigh, and open my eyes again, wishing I could remember more and knowing I can't, feeling ever so better about my day because, for a second there, I do remember holding her and knowing that I was so very lucky to have been her little sunshine, in that ancient history, so long ago.

I turn my head and look at A-level art projects she inspired, punk pictures and song lyrics blue-tacked to the wall, showing where I came from and how I got here.

Ami Gray (b.1990)

The Only Time My Father Ever Smacked Me

It was a grey autumn day, not a breath of wind, no leaves on the trees and no birds singing. I wasn't at school. My school in Bushey Heath had been bombed the week before, so there was no longer a school to go to. A lovely happy school—gone for ever.

Day pupils like me, who went home every day after school, had not yet been allocated a new school. The other pupils, those whose parents were stationed abroad and who lived at the school, had been transferred to another boarding school in Cornwall in the west of England, well away from the bombing. Several of my friends had been sent to Cornwall, and today other girls that I knew were out shopping with their mothers.

I was bored with nothing to do. The air raid siren sounded but no enemy planes flew overhead. Feeling there was no danger after several minutes with no enemy planes in sight, I left my parent's garden and went through the gap in the fence into the neighbour's orchard.

Besides the various trees: apple, pear, plum and damson, the orchard also had hazelnut hedges and a selection of fruit bushes. It was a wonderful place to play in with friends. The neighbours were very kind and had allowed my father to hang a swing from their walnut tree. But swinging back and forth on my own with only myself to talk to was still boring.

A little while after the air raid siren had sounded my mother realised I wasn't in the house, nor had I gone to the safety of our air raid shelter situated in the garden. Becoming concerned she walked over to the repair garage that my father owned and told him that she didn't know where I was. He stopped work and went to look for me in the garden calling my name. When I didn't answer he came through into the orchard.

I saw him before he saw me, and for a prank hid behind a large tree trunk. While he searched and called I made sure I was always on the far side of the tree so that he wouldn't see me. After a while my father left to look elsewhere. With my boredom gone, I nipped back into our own garden to see my guinea pigs. They had a hutch in a corrugated iron shed that protected them from the shrapnel that fell from the sky when German and British aircraft were fighting high above.

Suddenly my anxious father was at my side. He grabbed my hand firmly and led me indoors. "Sit down over there," he said sharply, pointing to a chair by the fire.

"No!" I replied and defiantly ran round the table and up the stairs.

Really angry now because of the unnecessary worry I had caused him and my mother, he followed me to my bedroom and smacked me, once, very hard for being so disobedient. Neither he or my mother had ever smacked me before, nor did they ever again. It was so against their nature. It was several days before I forgave him for what at the time I saw as an injustice.

But later as a grown up and parent myself I realised how much worry and distress I had caused them both.

As told to Tony Tucker by Elizabeth Payn (Note there is no 'e' in the name)

Wartime Shopping

I was born in 1932 and so spent much of my childhood during the Second World War and afterwards. Shopping was very difficult, because everything was in short supply.

You had to queue for many things and, as my mother was so busy, she used to send me to do the shopping. I hated queuing and have done so ever since!

We had ration books, of course, and we had something like one piece of meat a week each, one egg each, a piece of cheese about 8" by 3" and so on. Nothing was packaged and very little was wrapped up.

Sugar was weighed out from a big tin and put into blue paper bags. Sweets were weighed and put into little white paper bags and you had about six sweets per person per week. Even when I got older, the rustle of white paper used to make me think of sweets!

Biscuits came to the shops in tins and were weighed out – the broken ones were cheaper. Fish and chips were always wrapped in white paper and then newspaper. People used to say it made them taste better!

Because I used to do the shopping, I remember some of the prices even now. Milk was 2d a pint and bread was 4d a loaf. Beetroots were sold raw and by the pound weight: 4d a pound. All potatoes and other root vegetables were dirty then; nothing was washed, so you often paid for the mud too!

There were 240d in £1 and, when I went out to work at 14 years of age, I earned £3.10/- a week.

All shops were individually owned, except for a few chain stores, like The Home & Colonial Stores or Sainsbury's. Where we lived, they were all privately-owned shops, and everyone knew everyone else.

Rationing continued long after the war ended and, indeed, some foods were in less supply after the war than during it. But everyone got some food – there was no black market, at least not where we lived.

It was not until the 1950s that washing powders and washing-up liquid came in. These products were wonderful and made a lot of difference to the life of the average housewife.

Then supermarkets started to arrive. At first, they were in towns. It was not until 1970 that the 'out of town' ones were built. Supermarkets started to sell things in bulk, in threes, sixes or dozens, and in larger containers, which worked out cheaper for the large consumer, but did not do a lot for singles or elderly people.

There was no delivery service as there had been before the war. We used to have our milk delivered and my mother-in-law used to have her whole week's shopping delivered by the Home and Colonial Stores. Nowadays, home delivery, by way of the Internet, is just about coming back.

The main differences between shopping today and when I was a young person are in the packaging. I think there is too much of it today and most is not necessary and wasteful of our resources.

Today, you can buy ready-made meals, whereas in the past everything had to be freshly-cooked, except perhaps for salad cream and a few things like that. We had no frozen food then – not until the 1970s.

Today you pay by credit card (if you are daft enough). But it was all cash then. So if you didn't have enough, you didn't buy. Simple as that.

Today there is a large range of everything on the shelves. Look at cereals; there were just cornflakes, shredded wheat and Weetabix when I was a child. Of course the poor man's standby was porridge, which is still the finest and most nutritious cereal that you will ever find in the world, so don't knock it.

When I went shopping, I had to carry a cane basket, which was lighter than a wooden one, but quite heavy to start with compared to today's plastic carrier bags.

I used to cycle to the shops and had a cane carrier on the front of my bike. Today, I go by car.

Today, there are labels on most foods, telling you what is in them.

194

These labels were quite simple when I was young: just the name of the product inside the jar, the weight of the contents, and name and address of the supplier.

These days, food comes from all over the world and the choice is endless. This means the use of a lot of aeroplanes to bring tomatoes from Mexico or apples from South Africa. When I was a child most food was home-grown, except for some tinned meats which came slowly by ship from New Zealand or Argentina. Corn often came from Canada and went straight to the flour mills.

I would not like to go back to the 1940s or 50s but I do think we have gone too far today and have more choice than is necessary. I wish we could send more food to those people who have not enough. I think there is some kind of imbalance in the world.

Angela Spencer-Harper b.1932

Wellington Walkabout

A report of the Wellington Walk for dogs and their owners: May 1990

It was 10.am with the promising haze of a glorious day ahead. People and dogs of assorted shapes and sizes were gathered at the starting point. A handsome German Shepherd was already sporting a blue rosette. He must have been assured of his Bonios, or was maybe a Cruft's champion. Mum and I were right at the back of the group; we didn't have a dog and couldn't quite see what was going on up front – but someone blew a whistle and we seemed to be off.

There was a silver lake to our right, complete with Canada geese. Distant trees appeared dark, blueish-green. The canine walkers invariably tried to outdistance their owners; they saw no need to save energy, though some showed a passing interest in a pen of domestic geese. This caused a great deal of indignant honking, but the ruffled birds were quickly left behind.

We were circling the lake. The ground was soft and springy. Everyone was in good humour. Mum said she could walk for miles.

'Well, that's the general idea,' I reminded.

We came upon an iguanodon (statue), resplendent in red. This was duly photographed by several people including Mum. A little boy informed us that this was a tyrannosaurus, but his dad could read better.

A little further along, we discovered an oxaeyana – a cross between an ox and a hyena? It looked sort-of like a dog and turned out to be an avid hunter of prehistoric horses. Poor little things! (as they were back then).

Brambles were trailing in the lake, and to the left was a cut off swampy patch with bulrushes and sadly sunken trees. Next came a small grove of baby Scots pine – much prettier.

And we'd done a mile!

There was still an eternal expanse of lake to the right. We overtook the next cluster of walkers, including a doberman and a wheezing spaniel. I noted the drumming of a distant woodpecker, and Mum recognised the misplaced crowing of a cockerel. She thought he must've overslept, but as I quickly pointed out, a rooster can crow when it feels like; it doesn't have to be dawn.

A microlite aircraft sailed above; that should've been viewed through binoculars and its number recorded, but at the age of fourteen, I didn't possess any. Eyes down to cross a wooden bridge over a trickle, hardly worthy to be called a stream.

And it was two miles.

That part of the lake was tranquil and mirror-like. A blackbird chortled from nearby woods. Here we saw the first evidence of storm damage: piles of fallen branches had been cleared to the side of the path. The miniature railway track now appeared on our left and, across the lake, a marina with gaily-coloured boats. We moved to avoid an approaching Landrover, and photographed the pint-sized engines. More walkers caught up, and a lost, black dog limped towards them. Someone stopped to rescue him.

We passed an adventure playground, and there was an oasis in the form of a small cafeteria. We decided we both deserved an ice-cream.

Several dogs and children were playing on a strangely pitted hillock. Mum wondered what had made the holes. 'Moles?' she suggested.

'Moles make bumps,' I informed. 'More likely rabbits.'

'Or a meteorite shower,' she quipped.

The path U-turned and took us back to the adventure playground.

And it was three miles.

We were approaching woods. Defoliated conifers stood forlorn among their lost finery. The raucous cry of a jackdaw sounded from the trees; and there was Catweazle's water tower (if anyone but Mum can remember him). A white boxer marched past with its owner in tow.

We were on the woodland path with soft leaf-mould underfoot. We crossed another bridge (more like a plank) over an even smaller trickle. There was seemingly endless electric fencing to border the deer park, but not a single deer in sight. Didn't really blame them; all those marching intruders didn't exactly encourage social interaction between deer and humans.

Now the path resembled wood chippings. The day grew warmer beyond the sun-dappled shade. There were no other walkers in sight, but the drone of light aircraft reminded us that civilization wasn't far away. The still-brown trees showed only a sprinkled haze of spring green (Mum always calls this 'wearing the green veil'). Then the sudden rich emerald of a solitary laurel startled the eye.

The trail had turned to mud with deep tyre tracks and unexpected sqidginess. We decided the Wellington Walk was aptly named as we wished we had worn them.

Close to the edge of the wood: a pair of tragically uprooted silver birch. But one of these had proved a useful perch for a couple of weary walkers. We saw the three and a half mile sign.

We were out in the open again: a wide, oak-studded park. The sun had reached full strength and I was glad I didn't wear a jacket. Mum removed hers and tied it around her middle. We were beginning to feel the strain, but took comfort in the thought that it wasn't far to the halfway point and sandwiches. The moss-ridden turf was springy and walking much easier, but Mum's calf muscles were still protesting.

Four miles and we were back in the woods. There was a cattle grid in the mud. Mum thought it looked like a cruel contraption. 'Does it trip up the poor dears and break their ankles?' She wondered aloud.

I said I didn't know. She said that made a change. 'But there's no 'S' on deer,' I added.

Mum was too puffed to argue.

We passed through a double iron gate and walked alongside more electric fencing. A trail of last year's beech mast crunched underfoot. Twisted wreckage of trees on the right – more storm damage. Was sure we must reach halfway soon...

Half-an-hour further on, Mum almost twisted her ankle on a partially interred root, then tripped over a small tree stump. We were tired, thirsty and hungry, but not quite defeated. Where was the marquee with its promise of free drinks?

I stopped to voice my worries. 'Something's wrong. We must've walked at least two miles since we saw the last sign.'

Mum said, 'Come to think of it, I haven't seen any blue arrows on trees for ages!'

'There's some people over there. Let's follow them!'

We raced through the trees. At least, I raced – Mum sort-of hobbled in pursuit. We had to jump a ditch to reach the other walkers. Mum didn't quite make it and her foot sank into the mud with an awful squelch. She later admitted to swearing in silence and with great restraint. I would have done the same, but loudly.

Having extricated her foot, amazingly still in its sneaker, we hurried to catch up the others. Strange – this lot didn't look any the worse for wear. Then we came to the two mile sign: again. We both stared at this with weary disbelief.

'Must have taken a wrong turn somewhere,' I stated the obvious.

We were lost.

Lawrence Palmer (b.1975)

Lightning Source UK Ltd.
Milton Keynes UK
UKHW011415030522
402369UK00004B/35